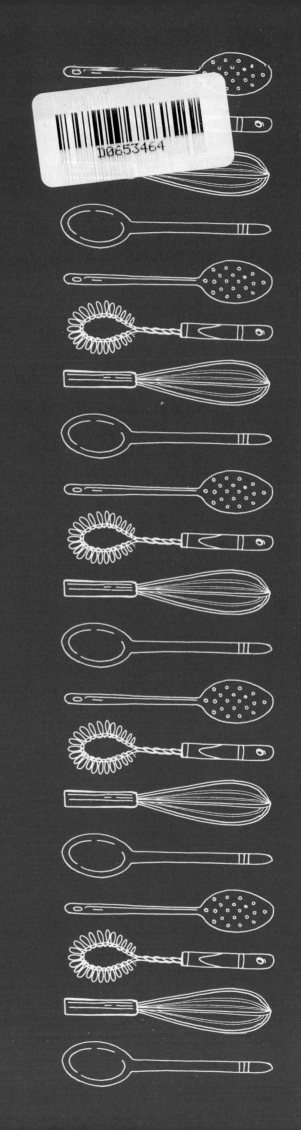

THE FAT-FREE COOKBOOK

THE FAT-FREE COOKBOOK

OVER 50 NUTRITIOUS AND TASTY FAT-FREE RECIPES, PERFECT FOR ANY OCCASION

CONSULTANT EDITOR ANNE SHEASBY

LORENZ BOOKS

This edition first published in 1998 by Lorenz Books

© Anness Publishing Limited 1998

Lorenz Books is an imprint of
Anness Publishing Limited
Hermes House
88–89 Blackfriars Road
London SE1 8HA

ISBN 1 85967 573 5

A CIP catalogue record for this book is available from the British Library

Publisher: Joanna Lorenz
Senior Cookery Editor: Linda Fraser
Editor: Margaret Malone
Designer: Ian Sandom
Nutritional Analysis: Wendy Doyle
Photography: Karl Adamson, Edward Allwright, Steve Baxter, James Duncan,
Amanda Heywood, Don Last, Patrick McLeavey, Michael Michaels,
Thomas Odulate and Peter Reilly
Recipes: Catherine Atkinson, Carla Capalbo, Kit Chan, Roz Denny, Christine
France, Shirley Gill, Christine Ingram, Sue Maggs, Annie Nichols, Maggie
Pannell, Laura Washburn and Stephen Wheeler

Printed and bound in Singapore

3 5 7 9 10 8 6 4 2

NOTES
For all recipes, quantities are given in both metric and imperial measures and,
where appropriate, measures are also given in standard cups and spoons.
Follow one set, but not a mixture, because they are not interchangeable.

Standard spoon and cup measures are level.
1 tsp = 5ml, 1 tbsp = 15ml, 1 cup = 250ml/8fl oz

Australian standard tablespoons are 20ml. Australian readers should
use 3 tsp in place of 1 tbsp for measuring small quantities of gelatine,
cornflour, salt, etc.

Size 3 (medium) eggs are used unless otherwise stated.

CONTENTS

INTRODUCTION

Cooking and eating good food is one of life's greatest pleasures – and there's nothing wrong with enjoying good food, except that for too long good often meant fatty. Butter, oil, cheese and other fatty foods were considered essential for good cooking. We know now that all this fat – along with too much sugar and salt – has a huge impact on health.

Most of us eat fats in one form or another every day. In fact, we need to consume a small amount of fat to maintain a healthy and balanced diet, but almost everyone can afford to, and should, reduce their fat intake, particularly of saturated fats. Weight for weight, dietary fats supply far more energy than all the other nutrients in our diet. If you eat a diet that is high in fats and don't exercise enough to use up

that energy, you will put on weight. By cutting down on fat, you can easily reduce your energy intake without affecting the other essential nutrients. And by choosing the right types of fat, using low fat and fat-free products whenever possible, and making small, simple changes to the way you cook and prepare food, you can reduce your overall fat intake quite dramatically and enjoy a much healthier diet without really noticing any difference.

As you will see, watching your fat intake doesn't have to mean dieting and deprivation. *The Fat-Free Cookbook* opens with an easy-to-follow informative introduction about basic healthy eating guidelines – you'll find out about the five main food groups, and how, by simply choosing a variety of foods from these groups every

day, you can ensure that you are eating all the nutrients you need. One way to enjoy your favourite foods without guilt is to substitute lower fat ingredients for higher fat ones. This book will introduce you to these lower fat ingredients and show you how to use them. There are hints and tips on how to cook with fat-free and low fat ingredients; techniques for using healthy, fat-free fruit purée in place of butter or margarine in all your favourite baking recipes; suggestions for which foods to cut down on and what to try instead; easy ways to reduce fat and saturated fat in your foods; new no fat and low fat cooking techniques and information on the best cookware for fat-free cooking; along with a delicious section on low fat and very low fat snacks.

There are over 50 easy-to-follow recipes for delicious dishes that your whole family can enjoy. Every recipe has been developed to fit into modern nutritional guidelines, and each one has at-a-glance nutritional information so you can instantly check the calories and fat content. The recipes are very low in fat – all contain less than five grams of fat per serving and many contain less than one. The selection of foods included will surprise you: there are barbecues and bakes, pizza and pastas, tasty sautés and stews, vegetable dishes and vegetarian main courses, fish and seafood dishes galore and delicious breads, biscuits and cakes. All without as much fat as traditional recipes, of course, but packed with flavour and vitality.

Fresh vegetables and pulses (far left) and fresh fruit (left and above) make ideal choices for fat-free and low fat cooking.

HEALTHY EATING GUIDELINES

A healthy diet is one that provides the body with all the nutrients it needs to be able to grow and repair properly. By eating the right types, balance and proportions of foods, we are more likely to feel healthy, have plenty of energy and a higher resistance to illness that will help protect our body against developing diseases such as heart disease, cancers, bowel disorders and obesity.

By choosing a variety of foods every day, you will ensure that you are supplying your body with all the essential nutrients, including vitamins and minerals, it needs. To get the balance right, it is important to know just how much of each type of food you should be eating.

There are five main food groups (see right), and it is recommended that we should eat plenty of fruit, vegetables (at least five portions a day, not including potatoes) and foods such as cereals,

pasta, rice and potatoes; moderate amounts of meat, fish, poultry and dairy products; and only small amounts of foods containing fat or sugar. By choosing a good balance of foods from these groups every day, and choosing lower fat or lower sugar alternatives wherever possible, we will be supplying our bodies with all the nutrients they need for optimum health.

THE ROLE AND IMPORTANCE OF FAT IN OUR DIET

Fats shouldn't be cut out of our diets completely. We need a small amount of fat for general health and well-being – fat is a valuable source of energy, and also helps to make foods more palatable to eat. However, if you lower the fats, especially saturated fats, in your diet, you will feel healthier; it will help you lose weight and reduce the risk of developing some diseases.

THE FIVE MAIN FOOD GROUPS

● Fruit and vegetables

● Rice, potatoes, bread, pasta and other cereals

● Meat, poultry, fish and alternative proteins

● Milk and other dairy foods

● Foods which contain fat and foods which contain sugar

Aim to limit your daily intake of fats to no more than 30% of total calories. In real terms, this means that for an average intake of 2,000 calories per day, 30% of energy would come from 600 calories. Since each gram of fat provides 9 calories, your total daily intake should be no more than 66.6g fat. Your total intake of saturated fats should be no more than 10% of the total calories.

TYPES OF FAT

All fats in our foods are made up of building blocks of fatty acids and glycerol and their properties vary according to each combination.

There are two types of fat – saturated and unsaturated. The unsaturated group is divided into two types – polyunsaturated and monounsaturated fats.

There is always a combination of each of the three types of fat (saturated, polyunsaturated and monounsaturated fats) in any food, but the amount of each type varies greatly from one food to another.

Left: By choosing a variety of foods from the five main food groups, you will ensure that you are supplying your body with all the nutrients it needs.

SATURATED FATS

All fatty acids are made up of chains of carbon atoms. Each atom has one or more free "bonds" to link with other atoms and by doing so the fatty acids transport nutrients to cells throughout the body. Without these free "bonds" the atom cannot form any links, that is to say it is completely "saturated". Because of this, the body finds it hard to process the fatty acid into energy, so it simply stores it as fat.

Saturated fats are the fats which you should reduce, as they can increase the level of cholesterol in the blood, which in turn can increase the risk of developing heart disease.

The main sources of saturated fats are animal products, such as meat, and fats, such as butter and lard that are solid at room temperature. However, there are also saturated fats of vegetable origin, notably coconut and palm oils, and some margarines and oils, which are processed by changing some of the unsaturated fatty acids to saturated ones – they are labelled "hydrogenated vegetable oil" and should be avoided.

POLYUNSATURATED FATS

There are two types of polyunsaturated fats, those of vegetable or plant origin (omega 6), such as sunflower oil, soft margarine and seeds, and those from oily fish (omega 3), such as herring, mackerel and sardines. Both fats are usually liquid at room temperature. Small quantities of polyunsaturated fats are essential for good health and are thought to help reduce the level of cholesterol in the blood.

MONOUNSATURATED FATS

Monounsaturated fats are also thought to have the beneficial effect of reducing the blood cholesterol level and this could explain why in some

Above: A selection of foods containing the three main types of fat found in foods.

Mediterranean countries there is such a low incidence of heart disease. Monounsaturated fats are found in foods such as olive oil, rapeseed oil, some nuts such as almonds and hazelnuts, oily fish and avocado pears.

CUTTING DOWN ON FATS AND SATURATED FATS IN THE DIET

About one quarter of the fat we eat comes from meat and meat products, one-fifth from dairy products and margarine and the rest from cakes, biscuits, pastries and other foods. It is easy to cut down on obvious sources of fat in the diet, such as butter, oils, margarine, cream, whole milk and full fat cheese, but we also need to know

about – and watch out for – "hidden" fats. Hidden fats can be found in foods such as cakes, biscuits and nuts. Even lean, trimmed red meats may contain as much as 10% fat.

By being aware of foods which are high in fats and particularly saturated fats, and by making simple changes to your diet, you can reduce the total fat content of your diet quite considerably. Whenever possible, choose reduced fat or low fat alternatives to foods such as milk, cheese and salad dressings, and fill up on very low fat foods, such as fruit and vegetables, and foods that are high in carbohydrate such as pasta, rice, bread and potatoes.

NATURE'S LOW FAT INGREDIENTS

Cutting down on fat doesn't mean sacrificing taste. It's easy to follow a healthy eating plan without having to forgo all your favourite foods. What is necessary, is to choose ingredients that are naturally lower in fat and prepare them with little – if any – additional fat. This is not as limiting as it sounds, as the following ingredients show.

FRUIT

● *Fresh Fruit* – Vitamin C is found almost exclusively in fruit and vegetables and because this vitamin cannot be stored by the body, levels need to be topped up continually. Fruits can be enjoyed raw or cooked: eat them raw in a salad; poach in fruit juice and serve hot with low fat yogurt or serve chunks on cocktail sticks as mini kebabs.

● *Dried Fruit* – A good selection of dried fruit is available including apples, apricots, bananas, currants, figs, kiwi fruit, mangoes, peaches, pears, prunes, pineapple, raisins and sultanas. Low in fat and high in dietary fibre, dried fruit makes a delicious healthy snack when you feel the need to nibble. Add to breakfast cereals, muesli or porridge and use in cake, biscuit and dessert recipes.

VEGETABLES

● *Fresh Vegetables* – These play an important part in a healthy, balanced diet. Valuable sources of vitamins and minerals, especially vitamins A, C and E, vegetables also contain lots of dietary fibre. Use frozen produce when fresh is not available – it is perfectly acceptable from a nutritional point of view.

Vegetables are often prepared using high fat methods. Below are just a few examples of everyday vegetables with some tips on how they can be prepared using low fat techniques.
Aubergines – Sprinkle with salt, soak for 30 minutes then rinse to draw out the juices and make them less spongy. Do not fry but brush lightly with oil and grill or blanch in boiling water.
Courgettes – Very absorbent, courgettes will soak up fat like a sponge if fried. Instead, cook in a tomato sauce, steam with a sprinkling of fresh herbs or

Above: Look no further than fresh fruit for a delicious and healthy snack.

thread chunks on to skewers and grill.
Mushrooms – Sweat in a little stock rather than butter or use raw in salads. Reconstituted dried mushrooms are excellent for adding an intense flavour to sauces, rice and pasta dishes.
Onions – An essential flavouring for many savoury dishes, sweat in stock or cook slowly with some red wine and herbs, rather than fry in oil.
Potatoes – High in carbohydrate, low in fat and containing some vitamin C and dietary fibre, especially if the skins are left on, potatoes are very valuable in terms of nutrition. Traditionally roasted or fried, try instead boiling, steaming or baking.

PASTA AND GRAINS

● *Oats and Oatmeal* – Just 50g/2oz of oats or oat bran a day, as part of a low fat diet, is known to dramatically reduce blood cholesterol. Oats and oatmeal come in a variety of types including porridge oats, quick-cook oats, jumbo oats, fine and medium oatmeal. Use them in muesli, oatcakes, mixed with flour for breads and rolls, in cakes and bakes and crumble toppings. Fine oatmeal also makes a good thickener for soups.

Left: Experiment with the wonderful range of fresh vegetables available today – you can't go wrong!

● *Pasta* – Containing very little fat, pasta is an ideal food on which to base a low fat diet. Pasta, like bread, potatoes, cereal, rice and most fruits, is high in filling "complex" carbohydrate, and when broken down by the body, it allows a steady release of energy to keep us satisfied for a long period of time. A nutritious and satisfying meal can be made simply by combining any pasta with a low fat sauce.

Pasta comes in a wide variety of shapes, colours and flavours. Don't worry if you can't find the exact variety suggested in a recipe, a general rule is that long strands such as spaghetti work best with thinner sauces, while short pasta shapes are good with chunky sauces. Sheets of pasta are ideal for layered dishes, and tiny shapes are added to soups.

● *Rice* – Like pasta, rice makes an ideal, versatile basis for a low fat diet. There are thousands of varieties of rice grown all over the world, with differing flavours and aromas. Choose from long-grain rice such as basmati, short-grain rice such as arborio and medium-grain rice. Brown rice, like all wholegrain cereals, has greater nutritional value, especially fibre.

The simplest way to cook rice is in a large quantity of boiling water, however valuable nutrients will be discarded in the leftover water. Try instead steaming or baking rice, allowing the rice to absorb all the water during the cooking.

BEANS AND PULSES

● *Fresh* – There are many varieties of fresh beans and pulses available, including peas, broad beans and runner beans and more unusual ones such as flageolet beans and black-eyed beans.

All are low in fat and are good sources of dietary fibre and contain

Above: Nutritious and versatile – pasta, rice, beans and pulses play a key role in a healthy low fat diet.

other nutrients including vitamins and minerals. Very versatile, they can be used in many dishes including salads, stir-fries, casseroles, pasta sauces, soups and curries. Some varieties, such as sugar-snap peas and mangetouts, can be eaten either raw or cooked.

● *Canned* – Varieties include black-eyed beans, butter beans, chick-peas, flageolet beans, lentils, peas and red kidney beans. Very nutritious and convenient to use, it is well worth having a few cans in your cupboard.

You can reduce the amount of meat used in a recipe by replacing it with some cooked pulses such as lentils, or try mashed cooked pulses as a good basis for dips.

● *Dried* – When buying, choose pulses that are plump and clear in colour and avoid broken, shrivelled or dusty beans. Pulses should be stored in a cool, dry place in an airtight container and used within one year.

Most dried pulses need to be soaked in water and then boiled until tender.

The older the beans are, the longer they will take to cook, and salt should be added at the end of the cooking time.

HERBS

● In cookery, herbs are used mainly for their flavouring and seasoning properties, as well as for adding colour and texture. By simply adding a single herb or a combination of herbs to food, everyday dishes can be transformed into delicious meals.

Herbs are very low in fat and calories and many, such as parsley, also provide useful vitamins and minerals.

POULTRY AND FISH

● A good source of quality protein, B vitamins and some iron, poultry is low in fat, particularly if the skin is removed. All fish is rich in protein, B vitamins and minerals, but choose white fish for its very low levels of fat. Grill or bake fish in the oven and sprinkle with lemon or lime juice and chopped fresh herbs.

FAT REDUCING TIPS

There are lots of simple no-fuss ways of reducing the fat in your diet. Just follow the simple "eat less – try instead" suggestions below to discover how easy it is.

● *Eat less* – Butter, margarine and hard fats.
● *Try instead* – Low fat spread or polyunsaturated margarine. If you must use butter or hard margarine, make sure they are softened at room temperature and spread them very thinly. Better still, use low fat spreads such as low fat soft cheese, reduced sugar jams or marmalades for sandwiches and toast.

● *Eat less* – Fatty meats and products such as meat pâtés, pies and sausages.
● *Try instead* – Low fat meats, such as chicken, turkey and venison.
    Use only the leanest cuts of such meats as lamb, beef and pork.
    Always cut any visible fat and skin from meat before cooking.
    Choose reduced fat sausages and meat products and eat fish more often.
    Try using low fat protein products such as Quorn or tofu in place of meat in recipes.
    Make gravies using vegetable water or fat-free stock rather than using meat juices.

● *Eat less* – Full fat dairy products such as whole milk, cream, butter, crème fraîche, whole milk yogurts and hard cheese.
● *Try instead* – Semi-skimmed or skimmed milk and milk products, low fat yogurts, low fat fromage frais and low fat soft cheeses, reduced fat hard cheeses such as Cheddar, and reduced fat creams and crème fraîche.

● *Eat less* – Deep-fried chips and sautéed potatoes.
● *Try instead* – Fat-free starchy foods such as pasta, couscous and rice. Choose baked or boiled potatoes.

● *Eat less* – Hard cooking fats, such as lard or hard margarine.
● *Try instead* – Polyunsaturated or monounsaturated oils such as olive, sunflower or corn for cooking.

● *Eat less* – Fried foods.
● *Try instead* – Fat-free cooking methods such as grilling, microwaving, steaming or baking whenever possible.
    Try cooking in a non-stick wok with only a very small amount of mono- or polyunsaturated oil.
    Always roast or grill meat or poultry on a rack.

● *Eat less* – High fat snacks such as crisps, tortilla chips, fried snacks and pastries, chocolate cakes, muffins, doughnuts, sweet pastries and biscuits – especially chocolate ones!
● *Try instead* – Low fat and fat-free fresh or dried fruits, breadsticks or vegetable sticks.
    Make your own home-baked low fat cakes and bakes.
    If you do buy ready-made cakes and biscuits, always choose low fat and reduced fat versions.

● *Eat less* – Rich salad dressings like full-fat mayonnaise, salad cream or French dressing.
● *Try instead* – Reduced fat or fat-free mayonnaise or dressings. Make salad dressings at home with low fat yogurt or fromage frais.

● *Eat less* – Added fat in cooking.
● *Try instead* – To cook with little or no fat. Use heavy-based or good quality non-stick pans, so that the food doesn't stick.
    Try using a small amount of spray oil in cooking to control exactly how much fat you are using.
    Use fat-free or low fat ingredients for cooking, such as fruit juice, low fat or fat-free stock, wine or even beer.

FAT-FREE COOKING METHODS

It's very easy to cook without fat – whenever possible, grill, bake, microwave or steam foods without the addition of fat, or try stir-frying without fat – use a little low fat or fat-free stock, wine or fruit juice instead.

● Choosing heavy-based or good quality cookware, you'll find that the amount of fat needed for cooking foods can be kept to an absolute minimum. When making casseroles or meat sauces such as bolognese, dry-fry the meat to brown it and then drain off all the excess fat before adding the other ingredients. If you do need a little fat for cooking, choose an oil which is high in unsaturates such as corn, olive, sunflower or rapeseed oil and always use as little as possible.

● When baking low fat cakes and bakes, use good quality bakeware which doesn't need greasing before use, or use non-stick baking paper and only lightly grease the tin before lining it.

● Look out for non-stick coated fabric sheet. This re-usable non-stick material is amazingly versatile, it can be cut to size and used to line cake tins, baking sheets or frying pans. Heat resistant up to 290°C/550°F and microwave safe, it will last for up to 5 years.

● When baking foods such as chicken or fish, rather than adding a knob of butter, try baking the food in a loosely sealed parcel of foil or greaseproof paper and adding some wine or fruit juice and herbs or spices before sealing the parcel.

● When grilling foods, the addition of fat is often unnecessary. If the food shows signs of drying, lightly brush with a small amount of unsaturated oil such as sunflower or corn oil.

Above: Invest in a few of these useful items of cookware for easy fat-free cooking: non-stick cookware and accurate measuring equipment are essential.

● Microwaved foods rarely need the addition of fat, so add herbs or spices for extra flavour and colour.

● Steaming or boiling are easy, fat-free ways of cooking many foods, such as vegetables, fish and chicken.

● Try poaching foods, such as chicken, fish and fruit, in stock or syrup – it is another easy, fat-free cooking method.

● Try braising vegetables in the oven in low fat or fat-free stock, wine or simply water with the addition of some herbs.

● Sauté vegetables in low fat or fat-free stock, wine or fruit juice instead of fat or oil.

● Cook fresh vegetables in a covered saucepan over a low heat with only a little boiling water so they cook in their own juices.

● Marinate food such as meat or poultry in mixtures of alcohol, herbs or spices, and soy sauce, vinegar or fruit juice. This will help to tenderize the meat and add flavour, aroma and colour and, in addition, the marinade can be used to baste the food while it is cooking.

● When serving vegetables such as boiled potatoes, carrots or peas, resist the temptation to add a knob of butter or margarine. Instead, sprinkle with chopped fresh herbs, such as parsley and coriander, or ground spices, such as ginger.

COOKING WITH LOW FAT OR NON-FAT INGREDIENTS

Nowadays many foods are available in full fat and reduced fat or very low fat forms. In every supermarket you'll find a huge array of low fat dairy products, such as milk, cream, yogurt, hard and soft cheeses and fromage frais; reduced fat sweet or chocolate biscuits; reduced fat or fat-free salad dressings and mayonnaise; reduced fat crisps and snacks; low fat, half-fat or very low fat spreads; as well as such reduced fat ready-made food products as desserts.

Other foods, such as fresh fruit and vegetables, pasta, rice, potatoes and bread, naturally contain very little fat. Some foods, such as soy sauce, wine, cider, sherry, sugar, honey, syrup and jam, contain no fat at all. By combining these and other low fat foods you can create delicious dishes which contain very little fat.

Some low fat or reduced fat ingredients and products work better than others in cooking but often a simple substitution of one for another will work. The addition of low fat or non-fat ingredients, such as herbs and spices, also add plenty of extra flavour and colour to recipes.

LOW FAT SPREADS IN COOKING

There is a huge variety of low fat, reduced fat and half-fat spreads available in our supermarkets, along with some spreads that are very low in fat. Some are suitable for cooking, while others are only suitable for spreading.

Generally speaking, the very low fat spreads with a fat content of around 20% or less have a high water content and so are all unsuitable for cooking and are only suitable for spreading.

Low fat or half-fat spreads with a fat content of around 40% are suitable for spreading and can be used for some cooking methods. They are suitable for recipes such as all-in-one cake and biscuit recipes, all-in-one sauce recipes, sautéing vegetables over a low heat, choux pastry and some cake icings.

When using these low fat spreads for cooking, the fat may behave slightly differently to full fat products such as butter or margarine.

With some recipes, the cooked result may be slightly different, but will still be very acceptable. Other recipes will be just as tasty and successful. For example, choux pastry made using half- or low fat spread is often slightly crisper and lighter in texture than traditional choux pastry, and a cheesecake biscuit base made with melted half- or low fat spread combined with crushed biscuit crumbs, may be slightly softer in texture and less crispy than a biscuit base made using melted butter.

When heating half- or low fat spreads, never cook them over a high heat. Always use a heavy-based pan over a low heat to avoid the product burning, spitting or spoiling, and stir all the time. With all-in-one sauces, the mixture should be whisked continuously over a low heat.

Half-fat or low fat spreads are not suitable for shallow or deep-fat frying, pastry making, rich fruit cakes, some biscuits, shortbread, clarified butter and preserves such as lemon curd.

Remember that the keeping qualities of recipes made using half- or low fat spreads may be reduced slightly, due to the lower fat content.

Almost all dairy products now come in low fat or reduced fat versions.

Another way to reduce the fat content of recipes, particularly cake recipes is to use a fruit purée in place of all or some of the fat in a recipe.

Many cake recipes work well using this method but others may not be so successful. Pastry does not work well. Breads work very well, perhaps because the amount of fat is usually relatively small, as do some biscuits and bars, such as brownies and flapjacks.

To make the dried fruit purée to use in recipes, chop 115g/4oz ready-to-eat dried fruit and place in a blender or food processor with 75ml/5 tbsp water and blend to a roughly smooth purée. Then, simply substitute the same weight of this dried fruit purée for all or just some of the amount of fat in the recipe. The purée will keep in the fridge for up to three days.

You can use prunes, dried apricots, dried peaches, or dried apples, or substitute mashed fresh fruit, such as ripe bananas or lightly cooked apples, without the added water.

Above: A selection of cooking oils and low fat spreads. Always check the packaging of low fat spreads – for cooking, they must have a fat content of about 40%.

LOW FAT AND VERY LOW FAT SNACKS

Instead of reaching for a packet of crisps, a high fat biscuit or a chocolate bar when hunger strikes, choose one of these tasty low fat snacks to fill that hungry hole.

● A piece of fresh fruit or vegetable such as an apple, banana or carrot – keep chunks or sticks wrapped in a polythene bag in the fridge.

● Fresh fruit or vegetable chunks – skewer them on to cocktail sticks or short bamboo skewers to make them into mini kebabs.

● A handful of dried fruit such as raisins, apricots or sultanas. These also make a perfect addition to children's packed lunches or to school break snacks.

● A portion of canned fruit in natural fruit juice – serve with a spoonful or two of fat-free yogurt.

● One or two crisp rice cakes – delicious on their own, or topped with honey, or reduced fat cheese.

● Crackers, such as water biscuits or crisp breads, spread with reduced sugar jam or marmalade.

● A bowl of wholewheat breakfast cereal or no-added-sugar muesli served with a little skimmed milk.

● Very low fat plain or fruit yogurt or fromage frais.

● A toasted teacake spread with reduced sugar jam or marmalade.

● Toasted crumpet spread with yeast extract or beef extract.

MINIMIZING OIL IN COOKING

For fat-free or low fat cooking, it's best to avoid roasting and frying, both of which soak oil into the food. Choose instead to poach, grill, bake, steam or microwave, all of which are successful ways of cooking without adding fat.

Below are some further handy techniques that may be used for reducing or eliminating the amount of oil used in cooking. If you do need a little fat for cooking, choose an oil which is high in unsaturates, such as olive or sunflower oil.

TECHNIQUE	GOOD FOR	HOW TO
SWEATING VEGETABLES	Pan frying any vegetables, such as onions, mushrooms, carrots and celery, which would often be initially fried in oil or butter, as the basis of many savoury recipes.	Put the sliced vegetables into a non-stick saucepan or frying pan with about 150ml/¼ pint/⅔ cup light stock. Cover and cook for 5 minutes or until the vegetables are tender and the stock has reduced. If you like, add 15ml/1 tbsp dry wine or wine vinegar for a little piquancy and continue cooking for a further few minutes until the vegetables are dry and lightly browned.
MARINATING	Adding flavour as well as helping to tenderize and keep the food moist during cooking without adding any fat. Useful for meat, fish, poultry and vegetables. The marinade may also be used to baste the food while cooking or added to an accompanying sauce.	Soy sauce, vinegar, citrus juices and yogurt all make excellent fat-free marinade bases with herbs and spices added for extra flavour. Leave for at least 30 minutes, preferably overnight.
PARCEL COOKING	Fish, chicken, vegetables and fruit, allowing the food to cook in its own juices and the steam created, holding in all the flavour and nutrient value and eliminating the need for oil or fats.	Enclose food in individual foil or greaseproof parcels, add extra flavourings such as wine, herbs and spices, if liked, twist or fold parcel ends to secure and ensure juices can't run out, then either bake, steam or cook on a barbecue.
SEARING	Sealing the juices into meat and poultry. Even lean cuts trimmed of skin and visible fat contain some hidden fat, so adding extra fat isn't necessary.	Place the meat in a heavy-based pan over a moderate heat and cook on all sides until evenly browned all over. If the meat is particularly lean and sticks slightly, remove from the pan, brush or spray a little oil on to the pan's surface, heat then return the meat to the pan. Any excess fat that comes out of the meat may be drained off before continuing with the recipe.

LOW FAT STOCKS

A good home-made stock is invaluable in the kitchen, forming the basis for many soups, starters and main course dishes. Below are two low fat stock recipes which are economical and easy to make.

You could add poultry giblets to the chicken stock and vary the ingredients in the vegetable stock according to taste and availability. Both can be frozen until required; the chicken up to 6 months, the vegetarian up to 1 month.

CHICKEN STOCK

INGREDIENTS

Makes 1.5 litres/2¹/₂ pints/6¹/₄ cups
1kg/2¹/₄lb chicken wings or thighs, skinned
1 onion
2 whole cloves
1 bay leaf
1 sprig of thyme
3–4 sprigs of parsley
10 black peppercorns

1 Cut the skinned chicken into pieces, then put them into a large, heavy-based saucepan. Peel the onion and stick with the cloves. Tie the bay leaf, thyme, parsley and peppercorns in a piece of muslin and add to the saucepan together with the onion.

2 Pour in 1.75 litres/3 pints/7¹/₂ cups of cold water and bring slowly to simmering point. Skim off any scum with a slotted spoon, then continue to simmer very gently, uncovered, for 1¹/₂ hours. Strain the stock through a sieve into a large bowl and leave until cold.

3 When cold, remove with a spoon the layer of fat that will have set on the surface.

> **COOK'S TIP**
>
> To make fish stock, follow the recipe for chicken stock, substituting fish bones, heads or trimmings for the chicken, and let simmer for 20–30 minutes.

VEGETABLE STOCK

INGREDIENTS

Makes 1.5 litres/2¹/₂ pints/6¹/₄ cups
2 carrots
2 celery sticks
2 onions
2 tomatoes
10 mushroom stalks
2 bay leaves
1 sprig of thyme
3–4 sprigs of parsley
10 black peppercorns

1 Chop the carrots, celery, onions, tomatoes and mushroom stalks. Place them in a large heavy-based saucepan. Tie the remaining ingredients in a piece of muslin and add to the pan.

2 Pour in 1.75 litres/3 pints/7¹/₂ cups cold water. Slowly bring to simmering point. Continue to simmer very gently, uncovered, for 1¹/₂ hours.

3 Strain through a sieve into a large bowl and leave until cold. Chill until required, or freeze in usable amounts.

LOW FAT SAUCES

Sauces can introduce an unwelcome amount of fat into a recipe, so that dishes which start out low in fat may end up being served in a rich, high fat coating. Unfortunately, it is not possible to simply introduce a low fat spread into most sauce recipes. The traditional roux method for making a sauce won't work successfully using low fat spreads because of their high water content, which will evaporate on heating, leaving insufficient fat to blend with the flour. Below, however, are three quick and easy low fat cooking methods to use, plus some alternatives to classic sauces.

● The All-in-One Method:
Place 25g/1oz/2 tbsp each of low fat spread and plain flour in a saucepan with 300ml/¹/₂ pint/1¹/₄ cups skimmed milk. Bring to the boil, stirring continuously until the sauce is thickened and smooth.

● Using Stock to Replace Fat:
Sweat vegetables, such as onions and mushrooms, in a small amount of stock rather than frying in fat.

● Using Cornflour to Thicken:
Blend 15ml/1 tbsp cornflour with 15–30ml/1–2 tbsp cold water, then whisk into 300ml/¹/₂ pint/1¹/₄ cups simmering stock or milk, bring to the boil and cook for 1 minute, stirring continuously.

LOW FAT VARIATIONS OF CLASSIC SAUCES

● Mayonnaise – You can buy commercially made reduced-calorie mayonnaise or to make further fat and calorie savings, substitute half the stated quantity with low fat natural yogurt or low fat fromage frais. This works well for mayonnaise-based dips or sauces like Thousand Island, which have tomato purée or ketchup added.

● Hollandaise – This sauce is classically made with egg yolks, butter and vinegar and can't be made with low fat spreads. However, some fat saving can be made by using less butter and including buttermilk. Place 3 egg yolks in a bowl with the grated rind and 15 ml/1 tbsp juice from 1 lemon. Heat gently over a pan of water, stirring until thickened. Gradually whisk in 75g/3oz/ 6 tbsp softened butter, in small pieces, until smooth. Whisk in 45ml/3 tbsp buttermilk and season. Reserve for special occasions.
   Alternatively, flavour plain yogurt with a little French mustard and a little vinaigrette dressing and use to drizzle over asparagus.

● Vinaigrette Dressings – Buy reduced-calorie and oil-free dressings or, if you like the real thing, simply use less.

● Oil-Free Dressings – Whisk together 90ml/6 tbsp low fat natural yogurt and 30ml/2 tbsp freshly squeezed lemon juice, and season to taste with freshly ground black pepper. If you prefer, wine, cider or even orange juice could be used in place of the lemon juice. Add chopped fresh herbs, crushed garlic, mustard, honey, grated horseradish or other flavourings, if you like.

● Using Vegetable Purées for Thickening – Many recipes for sauces are traditionally thickened by adding cream, beurre manié (a butter and flour paste) or egg yolks, all of which add unwanted fat to the sauce. If cooked vegetables are included in the recipe, blend some down in a food processor to make a purée then stir back into the juices to produce a thickened sauce. Good for casserole sauces.

LOW FAT SWEET OPTIONS

Desserts needn't be banned from a low fat diet. Many traditional dairy products are high in fat but it's a simple matter to adapt recipes and use low fat alternatives to create delicious results. Below are some simple low fat alternatives to using real dairy whipped cream which can be served with puddings or used for decorating cakes and desserts. Strained yogurt is lower in fat than many commercial varieties and is delicious served with puddings.

LOW FAT WHIPPED CREAM

INGREDIENTS

Makes 150ml/¹/₄ pint/²/₃ cup
2.5ml/¹/₂ tsp powdered gelatine
75ml/5 tbsp cold water
50g/2oz/¹/₄ cup skimmed milk powder
15ml/1 tbsp caster sugar
15ml/1 tbsp lemon juice

1 Sprinkle the powdered gelatine over 15ml/1 tbsp of the water in a small bowl and leave to "sponge" for 5 minutes. Place the bowl over a saucepan of hot water and stir until dissolved. Leave to cool.

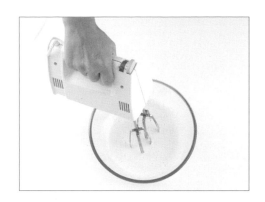

2 Whisk the milk powder, sugar, lemon juice and remaining water until frothy. Add the dissolved gelatine and whisk. Chill for 30 minutes.

3 Whisk the chilled mixture again until very thick and frothy. Serve within 30 minutes of making.

YOGURT PIPING CREAM

INGREDIENTS

Makes 450ml/³/₄ pint/scant 2 cups
10ml/2 tsp powdered gelatine
300ml/¹/₂ pint/1¹/₄ cups strained yogurt
15ml/1 tbsp sugar
2.5ml/¹/₂ tsp vanilla essence
1 egg white

1 Sprinkle the powdered gelatine over 45ml/3 tbsp cold water in a small bowl and leave to "sponge" for 5 minutes. Place the bowl over a saucepan of hot water and stir until dissolved. Leave to cool.

2 Mix together the yogurt, sugar and vanilla essence. Stir in the gelatine. Chill for 30 minutes, or until just beginning to set around the edges.

3 Whisk the egg white until stiff and carefully fold it into the yogurt mixture. Spoon into a piping bag and use immediately.

STRAINED YOGURT AND SIMPLE CURD CHEESE

• To make strained yogurt: line a nylon or stainless steel sieve with a double layer of muslin. Put over a bowl and pour in 600ml/1 pint/2¹/₂ cups low fat yogurt. Leave to drain in the fridge for 3 hours – it will have separated into thick strained yogurt and watery whey.
• To make curd cheese: leave the yogurt to drain for 8 hours or overnight. Spoon the curd cheese into a bowl, cover and chill until required. Use instead of soured cream, cream cheese or butter. Makes 115g/4oz/¹/₂ cup.

THE FAT AND CALORIE CONTENTS OF FOOD

The following figures show the weight of fat (g) and the energy content per 100g/3.5oz of each food.

VEGETABLES

	FAT (g)	ENERGY		FAT (g)	ENERGY
Broccoli	0.9	33 Kcals/138 kJ	Onions	0.2	36 Kcals/151 kJ
Cabbage	0.4	26 Kcals/109 kJ	Peas	1.5	83 Kcals/344 kJ
Carrots	0.3	35 Kcals/146 kJ	Potatoes	0.2	75 Kcals/318 kJ
Cauliflower	0.9	34 Kcals/142 kJ	Chips, home-made	6.7	189 Kcals/796 kJ
Courgettes	0.4	18 Kcals/74 kJ	Chips, retail	12.4	239 Kcals/1001 kJ
Cucumber	0.1	10 Kcals/40 kJ	Oven-chips, frozen, baked	4.2	162 Kcals/687 kJ
Mushrooms	0.5	13 Kcals/55 kJ	Tomatoes	0.3	17 Kcals/73 kJ

BEANS AND PULSES

	FAT (g)	ENERGY		FAT (g)	ENERGY
Black-eyed beans, cooked	1.8	116 Kcals/494 kJ	Hummus	12.6	187 Kcals/781 kJ
Butter beans, canned	0.5	77 Kcals/327 kJ	Red kidney beans, canned	0.6	100 Kcals/424 kJ
Chick-peas, canned	2.9	115 Kcals/487 kJ	Red lentils, cooked	0.4	100 Kcals/424 kJ

FISH AND SEAFOOD

	FAT (g)	ENERGY		FAT (g)	ENERGY
Cod fillets, raw	0.7	80 Kcals/337 kJ	Prawns	0.9	99 Kcals/418 kJ
Crab, canned	0.5	77 Kcals/326 kJ	Trout, grilled	5.4	135 Kcals/565 kJ
Haddock, raw	0.6	81 Kcals/345 kJ	Tuna, canned in brine	0.6	99 Kcals/422 kJ
Lemon sole, raw	1.5	83 Kcals/351 kJ	Tuna, canned in oil	9.0	189 Kcals/794 kJ

MEAT PRODUCTS

	FAT (g)	ENERGY		FAT (g)	ENERGY
Bacon rasher, streaky	39.5	414 Kcals/1710 kJ	Chicken fillet, raw	1.1	106 Kcals/449 kJ
Turkey rasher	1.0	99 Kcals/414 kJ	Chicken, roasted	12.5	218 Kcals/910 kJ
Beef mince, raw	16.2	225 Kcals/934 kJ	Duck, meat only, raw	6.5	137 Kcals/575 kJ
Beef mince, extra lean, raw	9.6	174 Kcals/728 kJ	Duck, roasted, meat, fat and skin	38.1	423 Kcals/1750 kJ
Rump steak, lean and fat	10.1	174 Kcals/726 kJ	Turkey, meat only, raw	1.6	105 Kcals/443 kJ
Rump steak, lean only	4.1	125 Kcals/526 kJ	Liver, lamb, raw	6.2	137 Kcals/575 kJ
Lamb chops, loin, lean and fat	23.0	277 Kcals/1150 kJ	Pork pie	27.0	376 Kcals/1564 kJ
Lamb, average, lean, raw	8.3	156 Kcals/651 kJ	Salami	45.2	491 Kcals/2031 kJ
Pork chops, loin, lean and fat	21.7	270 Kcals/1119 kJ	Sausage roll, flaky pastry	36.4	477 Kcals/1985 kJ
Pork, average, lean, raw	4.0	123 Kcals/519 kJ			

Information from *The Composition of Foods* (5th Edition 1991) is reproduced with the permission of the Royal Society of Chemistry and the Controller of Her Majesty's Stationery Office.

DAIRY, FATS AND OILS

	FAT (g)	ENERGY		FAT (g)	ENERGY
Cream, double	48.0	449 Kcals/1849 kJ	Low fat yogurt, plain	0.8	56 Kcals/236 kJ
Cream, single	19.1	198 Kcals/817 kJ	Greek yogurt	9.1	115 Kcals/477 kJ
Cream, whipping	39.3	373 Kcals/1539 kJ	Reduced fat Greek yogurt	5.0	80 Kcals/335 kJ
Crème fraîche	40.0	379 Kcals/1567 kJ	Butter	81.7	737 Kcals/3031 kJ
Reduced fat crème fraîche	15.0	165 Kcals/683 kJ	Margarine	81.6	739 Kcals/3039 kJ
Reduced fat double cream	24.0	243 Kcals/1002 kJ	Low fat spread	40.5	390 Kcals/1605 kJ
Milk, skimmed	0.1	33 Kcals/130 kJ	Very low fat spread	25	273 Kcals/1128 kJ
Milk, whole	3.9	66 Kcals/275 kJ	Lard	99.0	891 Kcals/3663 kJ
Brie	26.9	319 Kcals/1323 kJ	Corn oil	99.9	899 Kcals/3696 kJ
Cheddar cheese	34.4	412 Kcals/1708 kJ	Olive oil	99.9	899 Kcals/3696 kJ
Cheddar-type, reduced fat	15.0	261 Kcals/1091 kJ	Safflower oil	99.9	899 Kcals/3696 kJ
Cream cheese	47.4	439 Kcals/1807 kJ	Eggs	10.8	147 Kcals/612 kJ
Fromage frais, plain	7.1	113 Kcals/469 kJ	Egg yolk	30.5	339 Kcals/1402 kJ
Fromage frais, very low fat	0.2	58 Kcals/247 kJ	Egg white	Trace	36 Kcals/153 kJ
Skimmed milk soft cheese	Trace	74 Kcals/313 kJ	Fat-free dressing	1.2	67 Kcals/282 kJ
Edam cheese	25.4	333 Kcals/1382 kJ	French dressing	49.4	462 Kcals/1902 kJ
Feta cheese	20.2	250 Kcals/1037 kJ	Mayonnaise	75.6	691 Kcals/2843 kJ
Parmesan cheese	32.7	452 Kcals/1880 kJ	Mayonnaise, reduced calorie	28.1	288 Kcals/1188 kJ

CEREALS, BAKING AND PRESERVES

	FAT (g)	ENERGY		FAT (g)	ENERGY
Brown rice, uncooked	2.8	357 Kcals/1518 kJ	Digestive biscuit (plain)	20.9	471 Kcals/1978 kJ
White rice, uncooked	3.6	383 K/cals/1630 kJ	Reduced fat digestive biscuits	16.4	467 Kcals/1965 kJ
Pasta, white, uncooked	1.8	342 Kcals/1456 kJ	Shortbread	26.1	498 Kcals/2087 kJ
Pasta, wholemeal, uncooked	2.5	324 Kcal/1379 kJ	Madeira cake	16.9	393 Kcals/1652 kJ
Brown bread	2.0	218 Kcals/927 kJ	Fatless sponge cake	6.1	294 Kcals/1245 kJ
White bread	1.9	235 Kcals/1002 kJ	Doughnut, jam	14.5	336 Kcals/1414 kJ
Wholemeal bread	2.5	215 Kcals/914 kJ	Sugar, white	0	105 Kcals/394 kJ
Cornflakes	0.7	360 Kcals/1535 kJ	Chocolate, milk	30.3	520 Kcals/2214 kJ
Sultana bran	1.6	303 Kcals/1289 kJ	Chocolate, plain	29.2	510 Kcals/2157 kJ
Swiss-style muesli	5.9	363 Kcals/1540 kJ	Honey	0	288 Kcals/1229 kJ
Croissant	20.3	360 Kcals/1505 kJ	Lemon curd	5.1	283 Kcals/1202 kJ
Flapjack	26.6	484 Kcals/2028 kJ	Fruit jam	0	261 Kcals/1116 kJ

FRUIT AND NUTS

	FAT (g)	ENERGY		FAT (g)	ENERGY
Apples, eating	0.1	47 Kcals/199 kJ	Pears	0.1	40 Kcals/169 kJ
Avocados	19.5	190 Kcals/784 kJ	Almonds	55.8	612 Kcals/2534 kJ
Bananas	0.3	95 Kcals/403 kJ	Brazil nuts	68.2	682 Kcals/2813 kJ
Dried mixed fruit	0.4	268 Kcals/1114 kJ	Hazelnuts	63.5	650 Kcals/2685 kJ
Grapefruit	0.1	30 Kcals/126 kJ	Pine nuts	68.6	688 Kcals/2840 kJ
Oranges	0.1	37 Kcals/158 kJ	Walnuts	68.5	688 Kcals/2837kJ
Peaches	0.1	33 Kcals/142 kJ	Peanut butter, smooth	53.7	623 Kcals/2581 kJ

SOUPS AND STARTERS

The wide variety of fresh ingredients available today makes it easy to create tempting soups and starters that are filling, nutritious and low in fat. The recipes in this section are versatile and easy to prepare, as well as being delicious. Hearty home-made soups, such as Sweetcorn Chowder with Pasta Shells or Vegetable Minestrone, served with a chunk of fresh crusty bread, are perfect as a starter, snack or light meal. Take advantage of the huge variety of fresh fruits and herbs now available to create fragrant, colourful, virtually fat-free starters such as Melon, Pineapple and Grape Cocktail and Mussels with Thai Herbs.

SPLIT PEA AND COURGETTE SOUP

Rich and satisfying, this tasty and nutritious soup will warm a chilly winter's day.

INGREDIENTS

Serves 4

175g/6oz/1⅞ cups yellow split peas
1 medium onion, finely chopped
5ml/1 tsp sunflower oil
2 medium courgettes, finely diced
900ml/1½ pints/3¾ cups chicken stock
2.5ml/½ tsp ground turmeric
salt and black pepper

1 Place the split peas in a bowl, cover with cold water and leave to soak for several hours or overnight. Drain, rinse in cold water and drain again.

2 Cook the onion in the oil in a covered pan, shaking occasionally, until soft. Reserve a handful of diced courgettes and add the rest to the pan. Cook, stirring, for 2–3 minutes.

3 Add the stock and turmeric to the pan and bring to the boil. Reduce the heat, then cover and simmer for 30–40 minutes, or until the split peas are tender. Adjust the seasoning.

4 When the soup is almost ready, bring a large saucepan of water to the boil, add the reserved diced courgettes and cook for 1 minute, then drain and add to the soup before serving hot with warm crusty bread.

COOK'S TIP
For a quicker alternative, use split red lentils for this soup – they need no presoaking and cook very quickly. Adjust the amount of stock, if necessary.

NUTRITION NOTES

Per portion:

Energy	174Kcals/730kJ
Fat	2.14g
Saturated fat	0.54g
Cholesterol	0
Fibre	3.43g

CHILLED FRESH TOMATO SOUP

This effortless uncooked soup can be made in minutes.

INGREDIENTS

Serves 6
1.5kg/3–3½lb ripe tomatoes, peeled and
  roughly chopped
4 garlic cloves, crushed
30ml/2 tbsp balsamic vinegar
4 thick slices wholemeal bread
black pepper
low fat fromage frais, to garnish

1 Place the tomatoes in a blender with the garlic. Blend until smooth.

2 Pass the mixture through a sieve to remove the seeds. Stir in balsamic vinegar and season to taste with pepper. Put in the fridge to chill.

3 Toast the bread lightly on both sides. While still hot, cut off the crusts and slice the toast in half horizontally. Place on a board with the uncooked sides facing down and, using a circular motion, rub to remove any doughy pieces of bread.

COOK'S TIP
For the best flavour, it is important to use only fully ripened, flavourful tomatoes in this soup.

4 Cut each slice into four triangles. Place on a grill pan and toast the uncooked sides until lightly golden. Garnish each bowl of soup with a spoonful of fromage frais and serve with the Melba toast.

NUTRITION NOTES	
Per portion:	
Energy	111Kcals/475kJ
Fat	1.42g
Saturated Fat	0.39g
Cholesterol	0.16mg
Fibre	4.16g

SWEETCORN CHOWDER WITH PASTA SHELLS

Smoked turkey rashers provide a tasty, low fat alternative to bacon in this hearty dish. If you prefer, omit the meat altogether and serve the soup as is.

INGREDIENTS

Serves 4
1 small green pepper
450g/1lb potatoes, peeled and diced
350g/12oz/2 cups canned or frozen sweetcorn
1 onion, chopped
1 celery stick, chopped
a bouquet garni (bay leaf, parsley stalks and thyme)
600ml/1 pint/2½ cups chicken stock
300ml/½ pint/1¼ cups skimmed milk
50g/2oz small pasta shells
oil, for frying
150g/5oz smoked turkey rashers, diced
salt and black pepper
bread sticks, to serve

1 Halve the green pepper, then remove the stalk and seeds. Cut the flesh into small dice, cover with boiling water and stand for 2 minutes. Drain and rinse.

NUTRITION NOTES

Per portion:
Energy	215Kcals/904kJ
Fat	1.6g
Saturated Fat	0.3g
Cholesterol	13mg
Fibre	2.8g

2 Put the potatoes into a saucepan with the sweetcorn, onion, celery, green pepper, bouquet garni and stock. Bring to the boil, cover and simmer for 20 minutes until tender.

3 Add the milk and season with salt and pepper. Process half of the soup in a food processor or blender and return to the pan with the pasta shells. Simmer for 10 minutes.

4 Fry the turkey rashers in a non-stick frying pan for 2–3 minutes. Stir into the soup. Season to taste and serve with bread sticks.

VEGETABLE MINESTRONE

INGREDIENTS

Serves 6–8

large pinch of saffron strands
1 onion, chopped
1 leek, sliced
1 stick celery, sliced
2 carrots, diced
2–3 garlic cloves, crushed
600ml/1 pint/2½ cups chicken stock
2 x 400g/14oz cans chopped tomatoes
50g/2oz/½ cup frozen peas
50g/2oz soup pasta (anellini)
5ml/1 tsp caster sugar
15ml/1 tbsp chopped fresh parsley
15ml/1 tbsp chopped fresh basil
salt and black pepper

1 Soak the pinch of saffron strands in 15ml/1 tbsp boiling water. Leave to stand for 10 minutes.

2 Meanwhile, put the prepared onion, leek, celery, carrots and garlic into a large pan. Add the chicken stock, bring to the boil, cover and simmer for about 10 minutes.

3 Add the canned tomatoes, the saffron with its liquid and the frozen peas. Bring back to the boil and add the soup pasta. Simmer for 10 minutes until tender.

COOK'S TIP
Saffron strands aren't essential for this soup, but they give a wonderful delicate flavour, with the bonus of a lovely rich orange-yellow colour.

4 Season with sugar, salt and pepper to taste. Stir in the chopped herbs just before serving.

NUTRITION NOTES	
Per portion:	
Energy	87Kcals/367kJ
Fat	0.7g
Saturated Fat	0.1g
Cholesterol	0
Fibre	3.3g

SALMON PARCELS

Serve these little savoury parcels just as they are for a snack, or with a pool of fresh tomato sauce for a special starter.

INGREDIENTS

Makes 12
90g/3½oz can red or pink salmon
15ml/1 tbsp chopped fresh coriander
4 spring onions, finely chopped
4 sheets filo pastry
sunflower oil, for brushing
spring onions and salad leaves, to
  serve

COOK'S TIP
When you are using filo pastry, it is important to prevent it drying out; cover any you are not using with a tea towel or cling film.

---

1 Preheat the oven to 200°C/400°F/ Gas 6. Lightly oil a baking sheet. Drain the salmon, discarding any skin and bones, then place in a bowl.

2 Flake the salmon with a fork and mix with the fresh coriander and spring onions.

3 Place a single sheet of filo pastry on a work surface and brush lightly with oil. Place another sheet on top. Cut into six squares, about 10cm/4in. Repeat with the remaining pastry, to make 12 squares.

4 Place a spoonful of the salmon mixture on to each square. Brush the edges of the pastry with oil, then draw together, pressing to seal. Place the pastries on a baking sheet and bake for 12–15 minutes, until golden. Serve warm, with spring onions and salad.

NUTRITION NOTES

Per portion:
Energy	25Kcals/107kJ
Fat	1.16g
Saturated fat	0.23g
Cholesterol	2.55mg
Fibre	0.05g

TOMATO CHEESE TARTS

These crisp little tartlets are easier to make than they look. Best eaten fresh from the oven.

INGREDIENTS

Serves 4
2 sheets filo pastry
1 egg white
115g/4oz/½ cup skimmed milk soft
  cheese
handful fresh basil leaves
3 small tomatoes, sliced
salt and black pepper

1 Preheat the oven to 200°C/400°F/ Gas 6. Brush the sheets of filo pastry lightly with egg white and cut into sixteen 10 cm/4 in squares.

2 Layer the squares in twos, in eight patty tins. Spoon the cheese into the pastry cases. Season with black pepper and top with basil leaves.

3 Arrange tomatoes on the tarts, add seasoning and bake for 10-12 minutes, until golden. Serve warm.

NUTRITION NOTES

Per portion:
Energy	50Kcals/210kJ
Fat	0.33g
Saturated fat	0.05g
Cholesterol	0.29mg
Fibre	0.25g

MELON, PINEAPPLE AND GRAPE COCKTAIL

A light, refreshing fruit salad, with no added sugar and virtually no fat, perfect for breakfast or brunch – or any time.

INGREDIENTS

Serves 4
½ melon
225g/8oz fresh pineapple or 225g/8oz
  can pineapple chunks in own juice
225g/8oz seedless white grapes, halved
120ml/4fl oz/½ cup white grape juice
fresh mint leaves, to decorate (optional)

1 Remove the seeds from the melon half and use a melon baller to scoop out even-size balls.

2 Using a sharp knife, cut the skin from the pineapple and discard. Cut the fruit into bite-size chunks.

3 Combine all the fruits in a glass serving dish and pour over the juice. If you are using canned pineapple, measure the drained juice and make it up to the required quantity with the grape juice.

4 If not serving immediately, cover and chill. Serve decorated with mint leaves, if liked.

COOK'S TIP
A melon is ready to eat when it smells sweet even through its thick skin. Use a firm-fleshed fruit, such as a Galia or honey-dew melon.

NUTRITION NOTES	
Per portion:	
Energy	79Kcals/331kJ
Fat	0.2g
Saturated Fat	0
Cholesterol	0
Fibre	1.1g

CHILLI TOMATO SALSA

This universal dip is great served with absolutely anything and can be made up to 24 hours in advance.

INGREDIENTS

Serves 4
1 shallot, peeled and halved
2 garlic cloves, peeled
handful of fresh basil leaves
500g/1¼ lb ripe tomatoes
10ml/2 tsp olive oil
2 green chillies
salt and black pepper

1 Place the shallot and garlic in a food processor with the fresh basil. Whizz the shallot, garlic and basil until finely chopped.

2 Halve the tomatoes and add to the food processor. Pulse the machine until the mixture is well blended and coarsely chopped.

3 With the motor running, slowly pour in the olive oil. Add salt and pepper to taste.

NUTRITION NOTES

Per portion:	
Energy	28Kcals/79kJ
Fat	0.47g
Saturated Fat	0.13g
Cholesterol	0
Fibre	1.45g

4 Halve the chillies lengthways and remove the seeds. Finely slice the chillies widthways into tiny strips and stir into the tomato salsa. Serve at room temperature.

COOK'S TIP
The salsa is best made in the summer when tomatoes are at their best. In winter, use a drained 400g/14oz can of plum tomatoes.

MUSSELS WITH THAI HERBS

Another simple dish to prepare. The lemon grass adds a refreshing tang to the mussels.

INGREDIENTS

Serves 6

1kg/2¼ lb mussels, cleaned and beards removed
2 lemon grass stalks, finely chopped
4 shallots, chopped
4 kaffir lime leaves, roughly torn
2 red chillies, sliced
15ml/1 tbsp fish sauce
30ml/2 tbsp lime juice
2 spring onions, chopped, and coriander leaves, to garnish

1 Put all the ingredients, except the spring onions and coriander, in a large saucepan and stir thoroughly.

2 Cover and cook for 5–7 minutes, shaking the saucepan occasionally, until the mussels open. Discard any mussels that do not open.

3 Transfer the cooked mussels to a serving platter.

4 Garnish the mussels with chopped spring onions and coriander leaves. Serve immediately.

NUTRITION NOTES	
Per portion:	
Energy	56Kcals/238kJ
Fat	1.22g
Saturated Fat	0.16g
Cholesterol	0.32mg
Fibre	0.27g

TOMATO PESTO TOASTIES

Ready-made pesto is high in fat but, as its flavour is so powerful, it can be used in very small amounts with good effect, as in these tasty toasties.

INGREDIENTS

Serves 2
2 thick slices crusty bread
*45ml/3 tbsp skimmed milk soft cheese
  or low fat fromage frais*
10ml/2 tsp red or green pesto
1 beef tomato
1 red onion
salt and black pepper

1 Toast the bread slices on a hot grill until golden brown on both sides turning once. Leave to cool.

2 Mix together the skimmed milk soft cheese and pesto in a small bowl until well blended, then spread thickly on to the toasted bread.

3 Cut the beef tomato and red onion, crossways, into thin slices using a large sharp knife.

4 Arrange the slices, overlapping, on top of the toast and season with salt and pepper. Transfer the toasties to a grill rack and cook under a hot grill until heated through, then serve immediately.

COOK'S TIP
Almost any type of crusty bread can be used for this recipe, but Italian olive oil bread and French bread will give the best flavour.

NUTRITION NOTES

Per portion:
Energy	177Kcals/741kJ
Fat	2.41g
Saturated fat	0.19g
Cholesterol	0.23mg
Fibre	2.2g

PASTA, PULSES AND GRAINS

Pasta, pulses and grains on their own are low in fat and a good source of carbohydrate, but they are often prepared with high fat ingredients and sauces. It is possible, however, to prepare appetizing low fat meals by creatively combining pasta, pulses and grains with flavourful ingredients and cooking them according to low fat guidelines. There are old favourites to choose from, including pasta classics such as Spaghetti alla Carbonara and Tagliatelle with Mushrooms, and new, exciting combinations, such as Minted Couscous Castles and Spicy Bean Hot Pot.

SPAGHETTI WITH CHILLI BEAN SAUCE

A nutritious vegetarian option, ideal as a low fat main course.

INGREDIENTS

Serves 6

1 onion, finely chopped
1–2 garlic cloves, crushed
1 large green chilli, seeded
  and chopped
150ml/¼ pint/⅔ cup vegetable stock
400g/14oz can chopped tomatoes
30ml/2 tbsp tomato purée
120ml/4fl oz/½ cup red wine
5ml/1 tsp dried oregano
200g/7oz French beans, sliced
400g/14oz can red kidney
  beans, drained
400g/14oz can cannellini
  beans, drained
400g/14oz can chick-peas, drained
450g/1lb spaghetti
salt and black pepper

NUTRITION NOTES	
Per portion:	
Energy	431Kcals/1811kJ
Fat	3.6g
Saturated Fat	0.2g
Cholesterol	0
Fibre	9.9g

1 To make the sauce, put the chopped onion, garlic and chilli into a non-stick pan with the stock. Bring to the boil and cook for 5 minutes until tender.

2 Add the tomatoes, tomato purée, wine, seasoning and oregano. Bring to the boil, cover and simmer the sauce for 20 minutes.

3 Cook the French beans in boiling, salted water for about 5–6 minutes until tender. Drain thoroughly.

4 Add all the beans and the chick-peas to the sauce and simmer for a further 10 minutes. Meanwhile, cook the spaghetti in a large pan of boiling, salted water according to the individual packet instructions, until *al dente*. Drain thoroughly. Transfer the pasta to a serving dish or plates and top with the chilli bean sauce.

> **COOK'S TIP**
> Rinse canned beans thoroughly under cold, running water to remove as much salt as possible and drain well before use.

SPAGHETTI ALLA CARBONARA

This is a variation on the classic charcoal burner's spaghetti, using turkey rashers and low fat cream cheese instead of the traditional bacon and egg.

INGREDIENTS

Serves 4

150g/5oz smoked turkey rashers
oil, for frying
1 medium onion, chopped
1–2 garlic cloves, crushed
150ml/¹/₄ pint/²/₃ cup chicken stock
150ml/¹/₄ pint/²/₃ cup dry white wine
200g/7oz low fat cream cheese
450g/1lb chilli and garlic-flavoured
  spaghetti
30ml/2 tbsp chopped fresh parsley
salt and black pepper
shavings of Parmesan cheese,
  to serve

1 Cut the turkey rashers into 1cm/¹/₂in strips. Fry quickly in a non-stick pan for 2–3 minutes. Add the onion, garlic and stock to the pan. Bring to the boil, cover and simmer for about 5 minutes until tender.

2 Add the wine and boil rapidly until reduced by half. Whisk in the cream cheese and season to taste.

4 Return the spaghetti to the pan with the sauce and parsley, toss well and serve immediately with a few thin shavings of Parmesan cheese.

COOK'S TIP
If you can't find chilli and garlic-flavoured spaghetti, use plain spaghetti and add a small amount of raw chilli and garlic in step 4 or use the pasta of your choice.

3 Meanwhile, cook the spaghetti in a large pan of boiling, salted water for 10–12 minutes until *al dente*. Drain thoroughly.

NUTRITION NOTES	
Per portion:	
Energy	500Kcals/2102kJ
Fat	3.3g
Saturated Fat	0.5g
Cholesterol	21mg
Fibre	4g

TAGLIATELLE WITH MUSHROOMS

Serves 4

1 small onion, finely chopped
2 garlic cloves, crushed
150ml/¼ pint/⅔ cup vegetable stock
225g/8oz mixed fresh mushrooms, such
*   as field, chestnut, oyster or*
*   chanterelles*
60ml/4 tbsp white or red wine
10ml/2 tsp tomato purée
15ml/1 tbsp soy sauce
5ml/1 tsp chopped fresh thyme
30ml/2 tbsp chopped fresh parsley, plus
*   extra to garnish*
225g/8oz fresh sun-dried tomato and
*   herb tagliatelle*
salt and black pepper
shavings of Parmesan cheese, to serve
*   (optional)*

1 Put the onion and garlic into a pan with the stock, then cover and cook for 5 minutes or until tender.

2 Add the mushrooms (quartered or sliced if large or left whole if small), wine, tomato purée and soy sauce. Cover and cook for 5 minutes.

NUTRITION NOTES

Per portion:

Energy	226Kcals/961kJ
Fat	1.5g
Saturated Fat	0.7g
Cholesterol	0
Fibre	2.9g

3 Remove the lid from the pan and boil until the liquid has reduced by half. Stir in the chopped fresh herbs and season to taste.

4 Cook the fresh pasta in a large pan of boiling, salted water for 2–5 minutes until *al dente*. Drain thoroughly and toss lightly with the mushrooms. Serve, garnished with parsley and shavings of Parmesan cheese, if you like.

RATATOUILLE PENNE BAKE

INGREDIENTS

Serves 6

1 small aubergine
2 courgettes, thickly sliced
200g/7oz firm tofu, cubed
45ml/3 tbsp dark soy sauce
1 garlic clove, crushed
10ml/2 tsp sesame seeds
1 small red pepper, seeded and sliced
1 onion, finely chopped
1–2 garlic cloves, crushed
150ml/¼ pint/⅔ cup vegetable stock
3 firm ripe tomatoes, skinned, seeded
   and quartered
15ml/1 tbsp chopped mixed herbs
225g/8oz penne or other pasta shapes
salt and black pepper
crusty bread, to serve

1 Wash the aubergine and cut into 2.5cm/1in cubes. Put into a colander with the courgettes, sprinkle with salt and leave to drain for 30 minutes.

2 Mix the tofu with the soy sauce, garlic and sesame seeds. Cover and marinate for 30 minutes.

3 Put the pepper, onion and garlic into a saucepan with the stock. Bring to the boil, cover and cook for 5 minutes until tender. Remove the lid and boil until all the stock has evaporated. Add the tomatoes and herbs to the pan and cook for a further 3 minutes, then add the rinsed aubergine and courgettes and cook until tender. Season to taste.

> **COOK'S TIP**
> Tofu is a low fat protein, but it is very bland. Marinating adds plenty of flavour – make sure you leave it for the full 30 minutes.

4 Meanwhile, cook the pasta in a large pan of boiling, salted water according to the packet instructions, until *al dente*, then drain thoroughly. Preheat the grill. Toss the pasta with the vegetables and tofu. Transfer to a shallow ovenproof dish and grill until lightly toasted. Serve with bread.

NUTRITION NOTES	
Per portion:	
Energy	208Kcals/873kJ
Fat	3.7g
Saturated Fat	0.5g
Cholesterol	0
Fibre	3.9g

BEAN PURÉE WITH GRILLED CHICORY

The slightly bitter flavours of the radicchio and chicory make a wonderful marriage with the creamy bean purée. Walnut oil adds a nutty taste, but olive oil could also be used.

COOK'S TIP
Other suitable pulses to use are haricot, mung or broad beans.

INGREDIENTS

Serves 4
400g/14oz can cannellini beans
45ml/3 tbsp low fat fromage frais
finely grated rind and juice of
  1 large orange
15ml/1 tbsp finely chopped
  fresh rosemary
4 heads of chicory
2 medium heads of radicchio
10ml/2 tbsp walnut oil
shreds of orange rind, to garnish
  (optional)

1 Drain the beans, rinse, and drain again. Purée the beans in a blender or food processor with the fromage frais, orange rind, orange juice and rosemary. Set aside.

2 Cut the heads of chicory in half lengthwise.

3 Cut each radicchio head into eight wedges. Preheat the grill.

4 Lay out the chicory and radicchio on a baking tray and brush with the walnut oil. Grill for 2–3 minutes. Serve with the purée and scatter over the orange shreds, if using.

NUTRITION NOTES	
Per portion:	
Energy	110Kcals/464kJ
Fat	2.5g
Saturated Fat	0.15g
Cholesterol	0.1mg
Fibre	5.3g

SPICY BEAN HOT POT

Serves 4

225g/8oz/3 cups button mushrooms
15ml/1 tbsp sunflower oil
2 onions, sliced
1 garlic clove, crushed
15ml/1 tbsp red wine vinegar
400g/14oz can chopped tomatoes
15ml/1 tbsp tomato purée
15ml/1 tbsp Worcestershire sauce
15ml/1 tbsp wholegrain mustard
15ml/1 tbsp soft dark brown sugar
250ml/8fl oz/1 cup vegetable stock
400g/14oz can red kidney
    beans, drained
400g/14oz can haricot or cannellini
    beans, drained
1 bay leaf
75g/3oz/½ cup raisins
salt and black pepper
chopped fresh parsley, to garnish

1 Wipe the mushrooms, then cut them into small pieces. Set aside.

2 Heat the oil in a large saucepan or flameproof casserole, add the onions and garlic and cook over a gentle heat for 10 minutes until soft.

3 Add all the remaining ingredients except the mushrooms and seasoning. Bring to the boil, lower the heat and simmer for 10 minutes.

4 Add the mushrooms and simmer for 5 minutes more. Stir in salt and pepper to taste. Transfer to warm plates and sprinkle with parsley.

NUTRITION NOTES	
Per portion:	
Energy	278Kcals/1169kJ
Fat	4.5g
Saturated Fat	0.55g
Cholesterol	0
Fibre	11.1g

VEGETABLE BIRYANI

This exotic dish made from everyday ingredients will be appreciated by vegetarians and meat-eaters alike. It is extremely low in fat, but packed full of exciting flavours.

INGREDIENTS

Serves 4–6

175g/6oz/1 cup long grain rice
2 whole cloves
seeds of 2 cardamom pods
450ml/¾ pint/scant 2 cups vegetable stock
2 garlic cloves
1 small onion, roughly chopped
5ml/1 tsp cumin seeds
5ml/1 tsp ground coriander
2.5ml/½ tsp ground turmeric
2.5ml/½ tsp chilli powder
1 large potato, peeled and cut into 2.5cm/1in cubes
2 carrots, sliced
½ cauliflower, broken into florets
50g/2oz French beans, cut into 2.5cm/1in lengths
30ml/2 tbsp chopped fresh coriander
30ml/2 tbsp lime juice
salt and black pepper
sprig of fresh coriander, to garnish

COOK'S TIP

Substitute other vegetables, if you like. Courgettes, broccoli, parsnip and sweet potatoes would all be excellent choices.

4 Preheat the oven to 180°C/350°F/ Gas 4. Spoon the spicy paste into a flameproof casserole and cook over a low heat for 2 minutes, stirring occasionally.

5 Add the potato, carrots, cauliflower florets, beans and 90ml/6 tbsp water. Cover and cook over a low heat for a further 12 minutes, stirring occasionally. Add the chopped coriander.

6 Remove the cloves and spoon the rice over the vegetables. Sprinkle over the lime juice. Cover and cook in the oven for 25 minutes, or until the vegetables are tender. Fluff up the rice with a fork before serving and garnish with a sprig of fresh coriander.

2 Reduce the heat, cover and simmer for 20 minutes, or until all the stock has been absorbed.

3 Meanwhile put the garlic cloves, onion, cumin seeds, coriander, turmeric, chilli powder and seasoning into a blender or coffee grinder together with 30ml/2 tbsp water. Blend to a smooth paste.

1 Put the rice, cloves and cardamom seeds into a large, heavy-based saucepan. Pour over the stock and bring to the boil.

COCONUT RICE

A delicious alternative to plain boiled rice, brown or white rice will both work well.

INGREDIENTS

Serves 6
450g/1lb/2 cups long grain rice
250ml/8fl oz/1 cup water
475ml/16fl oz/2 cups coconut milk
2.5ml/¹⁄₂ tsp salt
30ml/2 tbsp granulated sugar
fresh shredded coconut, to garnish

1 Wash the rice in cold water until it runs clear. Place the water, coconut milk, salt and sugar in a heavy-based saucepan or flameproof casserole.

COOK'S TIP
Coconut milk is available in cans, but if you cannot find it, use creamed coconut mixed with water according to the packet instructions.

2 Add the rice, cover and bring to the boil. Reduce the heat to low and simmer for about 15–20 minutes or until the rice is tender to the bite and cooked through.

3 Turn off the heat and allow the rice to rest in the saucepan for a further 5–10 minutes.

4 Fluff up the rice with chopsticks or a fork before serving garnished with shredded coconut.

NUTRITION NOTES

Per portion:

Energy	322.5Kcals/1371kJ
Fat	2.49g
Saturated Fat	1.45g
Cholesterol	0
Fibre	0.68g

MINTED COUSCOUS CASTLES

Couscous is a fine semolina made from wheat grain, which is usually steamed and served plain with a rich meat or vegetable stew. Here it is flavoured with mint and moulded to make an unusual accompaniment to serve with any savoury dish.

INGREDIENTS

Serves 6
225g/8oz/1¼ cups couscous
475ml/16 fl oz/2 cups boiling stock
15ml/1 tbsp lemon juice
2 tomatoes, diced
30ml/2 tbsp chopped fresh mint
oil, for brushing
salt and black pepper
mint sprigs, to garnish

1 Place the couscous in a bowl and pour over the boiling stock. Cover the bowl and leave to stand for 30 minutes, until all the stock is absorbed and the grains are tender.

2 Stir in the lemon juice with the tomatoes and chopped mint. Adjust the seasoning with salt and pepper.

3 Brush the insides of four cups or individual moulds with oil. Spoon in the couscous mixture and pack down firmly. Chill for several hours.

4 Turn out and serve cold, or alternatively, cover and heat gently in a low oven or microwave, then turn out and serve hot, garnished with mint.

COOK'S TIP
Most packet couscous is now the ready cooked variety, which can be cooked as above, but some types need steaming first, so check the pack instructions.

NUTRITION NOTES

Per portion:
Energy	95Kcals/397kJ
Fat	0.53g
Saturated fat	0.07g
Cholesterol	0
Fibre	0.29g

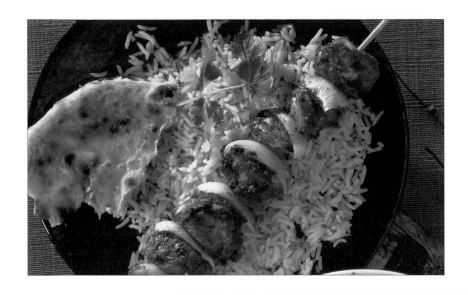

MEAT AND POULTRY

There is no reason why meat should not be a valuable part of a low fat diet. Make the most of the many leaner cuts of meat available today and utilize the low fat preparation and cooking methods to make delicious, low fat dishes. Most poultry, especially chicken and turkey, is naturally low in fat, making it ideal for a low fat diet. Included here are a wide range of tasty and nutritious main courses, all packed with flavour. Try Turkey and Pasta Bake, perfect for feeding a family; spicy Tandoori Chicken Kebabs for an al fresco summer lunch and Venison with Cranberry Sauce for a special occasion dinner.

CHICKEN, CARROT AND LEEK PARCELS

These intriguing parcels may sound a bit fiddly for everyday eating, but actually they take very little time, and you can freeze them ready to cook from frozen when needed.

INGREDIENTS

Serves 4
4 *chicken fillets or skinless, boneless breast portions*
2 *small leeks, sliced*
2 *carrots, grated*
2 *stoned black olives, chopped*
1 *garlic clove, crushed*
4 *anchovy fillets, halved lengthways*
salt and black pepper
black olives and herb sprigs, to garnish

1 Preheat the oven to 200°C/400°F/ Gas 6. Season the chicken well.

2 Cut out four sheets of lightly greased greaseproof paper about 23cm/9in square. Divide the leeks equally among them. Put a piece of chicken on top of each.

3 Mix the carrots, olives and garlic together. Season lightly and place on top of the chicken portions. Top each with two of the anchovy fillets.

4 Carefully wrap up each parcel, making sure the paper folds are sealed. Bake the parcels for 20 minutes and serve hot, in the paper, garnished with black olives and herb sprigs.

NUTRITION NOTES

Per portion:
Energy	154Kcals/651kJ
Fat	2.37g
Saturated Fat	0.45g
Cholesterol	78.75mg
Fibre	2.1g

COOK'S TIP
Skinless, boneless chicken is low in fat and is an excellent source of protein. Small, skinless turkey breast fillets also work well in this recipe and make a tasty change.

Ragoût of Veal

If you are looking for a low-calorie dish to treat yourself – or some guests – then this is perfect, and quick, too.

Ingredients

Serves 4
375g/12oz veal fillet or loin
10ml/2 tsp olive oil
10–12 tiny onions, kept whole
1 yellow pepper, seeded and cut into eighths
1 orange or red pepper, seeded and cut into eighths
3 tomatoes, peeled and quartered
4 fresh basil sprigs
30ml/2 tbsp dry martini or sherry
salt and black pepper

Nutrition Notes

Per portion:
Energy   158Kcals/665.5kJ
Fat   4.97g
Saturated Fat   1.14g
Cholesterol   63mg
Fibre   2.5g

2 After a couple of minutes, add the peppers and tomatoes. Continue stir-frying for another 4–5 minutes.

Cook's Tip
Lean beef or pork fillet may be used instead of veal, if you prefer. Shallots can replace the onions.

1 Trim off any fat and cut the veal into cubes. Heat the oil in a frying pan and gently stir-fry the veal and onions until browned.

3 Add half the basil leaves, roughly chopped (keep some for garnish), the martini or sherry, and seasoning. Cook, stirring frequently, for another 10 minutes, or until the meat is tender.

4 Sprinkle with the remaining basil leaves and serve hot.

VENISON WITH CRANBERRY SAUCE

Venison steaks are now readily available. Lean and low in fat, they make a healthy choice for a special occasion. Served with a sauce of fresh seasonal cranberries, port and ginger, they make a dish with a wonderful combination of flavours.

INGREDIENTS

Serves 4

1 orange
1 lemon
75g/3oz/1 cup fresh or frozen
  cranberries
5ml/1 tsp grated fresh root ginger
1 thyme sprig, plus extra to garnish
5ml/1 tsp Dijon mustard
60ml/4 tbsp redcurrant jelly
150ml/¼ pint/⅔ cup ruby port
10ml/2 tsp sunflower oil
4 x 90g/3½oz venison steaks
2 shallots, finely chopped
salt and black pepper
mashed potato and broccoli, to serve

NUTRITION NOTES

Per portion:	
Energy	250Kcals/1055.5kJ
Fat	4.39g
Saturated Fat	1.13g
Cholesterol	50mg
Fibre	1.59g

COOK'S TIP
When frying venison, always remember: the briefer the better. Venison will turn to leather if subjected to fierce heat after it has reached the medium-rare stage. If you dislike any hint of pink, cook it to this stage, then let it rest in a low oven for a few minutes.

1 Pare the rind from half the orange and half the lemon using a vegetable peeler, then cut into very fine strips.

2 Blanch the strips in a small pan of boiling water for about 5 minutes until tender. Drain the strips and refresh under cold water.

3 Squeeze the juice from the orange and lemon, then pour into a small pan. Add the cranberries, ginger, thyme sprig, mustard, redcurrant jelly and port. Cook over a low heat until the jelly melts.

4 Bring the sauce to the boil, stirring occasionally, then cover the pan and reduce the heat. Cook gently for about 15 minutes, until the cranberries are just tender.

VARIATION
When fresh cranberries are unavailable, use redcurrants instead. Stir them into the sauce towards the end of cooking with the orange and lemon rinds.

5 Heat the oil in a heavy-based frying pan, add the venison steaks and cook over a high heat for 2–3 minutes.

6 Turn over the steaks and add the shallots to the pan. Cook the steaks on the other side for 2–3 minutes, depending on whether you like rare or medium-cooked meat.

7 Just before the end of cooking, pour in the sauce and add the strips of orange and lemon rind.

8 Leave the sauce to bubble for a few seconds to thicken slightly, then remove the thyme sprig and adjust the seasoning to taste.

9 Transfer the venison steaks to warmed plates and spoon over the sauce. Garnish with thyme sprigs and serve accompanied by mashed potato and broccoli.

WARM CHICKEN SALAD

Succulent cooked chicken pieces are combined with vegetables in a light chilli dressing.

INGREDIENTS

Serves 6

50g/2oz mixed salad leaves
50g/2oz baby spinach leaves
50g/2oz watercress
30ml/2 tbsp chilli sauce
30ml/2 tbsp dry sherry
15ml/1 tbsp light soy sauce
15ml/1 tbsp tomato ketchup
10ml/2 tsp olive oil
8 shallots, finely chopped
1 garlic clove, crushed
350g/12oz skinless, boneless chicken
    breast, cut into thin strips
1 red pepper, seeded and sliced
175g/6oz mangetouts, trimmed
400g/14oz can baby sweetcorn, drained
    and halved lengthways
275g/10oz can brown rice
salt and ground black pepper
parsley sprig, to garnish

NUTRITION NOTES	
Per portion:	
Energy	190Kcals/801kJ
Fat	4.0g
Saturated Fat	0.91g
Cholesterol	25.1mg
Fibre	3.1g

1 Arrange the mixed salad leaves, tearing up any large ones, and the spinach leaves on a serving dish. Add the watercress and toss to mix.

2 In a small bowl, mix together the chilli sauce, sherry, soy sauce and tomato ketchup and set aside.

3 Heat the oil in a large non-stick frying pan or wok. Add the shallots and garlic and stir-fry over a medium heat for 1 minute. Add the chicken and stir-fry for 3–4 minutes.

4 Add the pepper, mangetouts, sweetcorn and rice and stir-fry for 2–3 minutes.

5 Pour in the chilli sauce mixture and stir-fry for 2–3 minutes, until hot and bubbling. Season to taste. Spoon the chicken mixture over the salad leaves, toss together to mix and serve immediately, garnished with a fresh parsley sprig.

TANDOORI CHICKEN KEBABS

This dish originates from the plains of the Punjab at the foot of the Himalayas, where food is traditionally cooked in clay ovens known as tandoors – hence the name.

INGREDIENTS

Serves 4

4 boneless, skinless chicken breasts
  (about 130g/3¹/₂oz each)
15ml/1 tbsp lemon juice
45ml/3 tbsp tandoori paste
45ml/3 tbsp low fat natural yogurt
1 garlic clove, crushed
30ml/2 tbsp chopped fresh coriander
1 small onion, cut into wedges and
  separated into layers
10ml/1 tsp oil, for brushing
salt and black pepper
fresh coriander sprigs, to garnish
pilau rice and naan bread, to serve

1 Chop the chicken breasts into 2.5cm/1in cubes, put in a bowl and add the lemon juice, tandoori paste, yogurt, garlic, coriander and seasoning. Cover and leave to marinate in the fridge for 2–3 hours.

2 Preheat the grill to high. Thread alternate pieces of chicken and onion on to four skewers.

COOK'S TIP
Use chopped, boned and skinned chicken thighs, or strips of turkey breasts, for a cheaper and equally low fat alternative.

3 Brush the onions with a little oil, lay the skewers on a grill rack and cook for 10–12 minutes, turning once.

4 Garnish the kebabs with coriander and serve at once with pilau rice and naan bread.

NUTRITION NOTES

Per portion:
Energy	215.7Kcals/911.2kJ
Fat	4.2g
Saturated Fat	0.27g
Cholesterol	122mg
Fibre	0.22g

SPAGHETTI BOLOGNESE

INGREDIENTS

Serves 8

1 onion, chopped
2–3 garlic cloves, crushed
300ml/½ pint/1¼ cups beef or
  chicken stock
450g/1lb extra-lean minced turkey
  or beef
2 x 400g/14oz cans chopped tomatoes
5ml/1 tsp dried basil
5ml/1 tsp dried oregano
60ml/4 tbsp tomato purée
450g/1lb button mushrooms, quartered
  and sliced
150ml/¼ pint/⅔ cup red wine
450g/1lb spaghetti
salt and black pepper

NUTRITION NOTES

Per portion:
Energy	321Kcals/1350kJ
Fat	4.1g
Saturated Fat	1.3g
Cholesterol	33mg
Fibre	2.7g

1 Put the chopped onion and garlic into a non-stick saucepan with half of the stock. Bring to the boil and cook for 5 minutes until the onion is tender and the stock has reduced completely.

> COOK'S TIP
> Sautéing vegetables in stock rather than oil is an easy way of saving calories and fat. Choose stock to reduce even more.

2 Add the turkey or beef and cook for 5 minutes, breaking up the meat with a fork. Add the tomatoes, herbs and tomato purée, bring to the boil, then cover and simmer for 1 hour.

3 Meanwhile, cook the mushrooms in a non-stick saucepan with the wine for 5 minutes or until the wine has evaporated. Add the mushrooms to the meat with salt and pepper to taste.

4 Cook the pasta in a large pan of boiling salted water for 8–12 minutes until tender. Drain thoroughly. Serve topped with the meat sauce.

TURKEY AND PASTA BAKE

INGREDIENTS

Serves 4

275g/10oz minced turkey
150g/5oz smoked turkey rashers,
  chopped
1–2 garlic cloves, crushed
1 onion, finely chopped
2 carrots, diced
30ml/2 tbsp tomato purée
300ml/¹/₂ pint/1¹/₄ cups chicken stock
225g/8oz rigatoni or penne pasta
30ml/2 tbsp grated Parmesan cheese
salt and black pepper

1 Brown the minced turkey in a non-stick saucepan, breaking up any large pieces with a wooden spoon, until well browned all over.

2 Add the chopped turkey rashers, garlic, onion, carrots, purée, stock and seasoning. Bring to the boil, cover and simmer for 1 hour until tender.

3 Preheat the oven to 180°C/350°F/Gas 4. Cook the pasta in a large pan of boiling, salted water according to the packet instructions, until *al dente*. Drain thoroughly and mix with the turkey sauce.

COOK'S TIP
Minced chicken or extra lean minced beef work just as well in this tasty recipe.

4 Transfer to a shallow ovenproof dish and sprinkle with grated Parmesan cheese. Bake for 20–30 minutes until lightly browned on top.

NUTRITION NOTES	
Per portion:	
Energy	391Kcals/1641kJ
Fat	4.9g
Saturated Fat	2.2g
Cholesterol	60mg
Fibre	3.5g

DUCK BREAST SALAD

Tender slices of succulent cooked duck breasts served with a salad of mixed pasta, fruit and vegetables, tossed together in a light dressing, ensure that this gourmet dish will impress friends and family alike.

INGREDIENTS

Serves 6

2 small duck breasts, boned
5ml/1 tsp coriander seeds, crushed
350g/12oz rigatoni or penne pasta
150ml/¼ pint/⅔ cup fresh orange juice
15ml/1 tbsp lemon juice
10ml/2 tsp clear honey
1 shallot, finely chopped
1 garlic clove, crushed
1 celery stick, chopped
75g/3oz dried cherries
45ml/3 tbsp port
15ml/1 tbsp chopped fresh mint, plus extra to garnish
30ml/2 tbsp chopped fresh coriander, plus extra to garnish
1 eating apple, diced
2 oranges, segmented
salt and black pepper

COOK'S TIP
Choose skinless duck breasts to reduce fat and calories. Crush your own spices, such as coriander seeds, to create fresh, aromatic, spicy flavours. Ready-ground spices lose their flavour more quickly than whole spices, which are best freshly ground just before use.

2 Cook the pasta in a large pan of boiling, salted water according to the packet instructions, until *al dente*. Drain thoroughly and rinse under cold running water. Leave to cool.

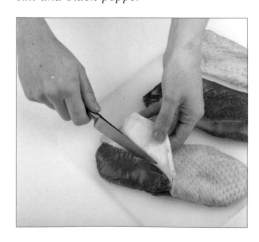

1 Remove the skin and fat from the duck breasts and season with salt and pepper. Rub with coriander seeds. Preheat the grill, then grill the duck for 10 minutes on each side. Wrap in foil and leave for 20 minutes.

3 To make the dressing, put the orange juice, lemon juice, honey, shallot, garlic, celery, cherries, port, mint and fresh coriander into a bowl, whisk together and leave to marinate for 30 minutes.

4 Slice the duck breasts very thinly. (They should be pink in the centre.)

5 Put the pasta into a large bowl, then add the dressing, diced apple and segments of orange. Toss well to coat the pasta. Transfer the salad to a serving plate with the duck slices and garnish with the extra mint and coriander.

NUTRITION NOTES	
Per portion:	
Energy	348Kcals/1460kJ
Fat	3.8g
Saturated Fat	0.9g
Cholesterol	55mg
Fibre	3g

FISH AND SEAFOOD

The range of fresh fish available in our supermarkets is impressive, and fish is always a good choice for a healthy low fat diet. Most fish, particularly white fish, is low in fat and is a good source of protein. Oily fish contains more fat than white fish, but contains high levels of essential fatty acids which are vital for good health. Fish is quick and easy to prepare and cook and is ideal for serving with fresh seasonal vegetables as part of a healthy low fat meal. Try Cajun-style Cod, Monkfish and Mussel Skewers or Curried Prawns in Coconut Milk — just some of the delicious, low fat recipes included in this chapter.

CAJUN-STYLE COD

This recipe works equally well with any firm-fleshed fish – choose low fat fish, such as haddock or monkfish.

NUTRITION NOTES

Per portion:
Energy	152Kcals/643kJ
Fat	1.9g
Saturated Fat	0.26g
Cholesterol	80.6mg
Fibre	0.1g

INGREDIENTS

Serves 4

4 cod steaks, each weighing about
175g/6oz
30ml/2 tbsp low fat natural yogurt
15ml/1 tbsp lime or lemon juice
1 garlic clove, crushed
5ml/1 tsp ground cumin
5ml/1 tsp paprika
5ml/1 tsp mustard powder
2.5ml/¹⁄₂ tsp cayenne pepper
2.5ml/¹⁄₂ tsp dried thyme
2.5ml/¹⁄₂ tsp dried oregano
non-stick cooking spray
lemon slices, to garnish
new potatoes and a mixed salad,
to serve

1 Pat the fish dry on kitchen paper. Mix together the yogurt and lime or lemon juice and brush lightly over both sides of the fish.

2 Mix together the crushed garlic, spices and herbs. Coat both sides of the fish with the seasoning mix, rubbing in well.

3 Spray a ridged grill pan or heavy-based frying pan with non-stick cooking spray. Heat until very hot. Add the fish and cook over a high heat for 4 minutes, or until the undersides are well browned.

4 Turn the steaks over and cook for a further 4 minutes, or until cooked through. Serve immediately, garnished with lemon and accompanied by new potatoes and a mixed salad.

PLAICE PROVENÇAL

INGREDIENTS

Serves 4
4 large plaice fillets
2 small red onions
120ml/4fl oz/¹/₂ cup vegetable stock
60ml/4 tbsp dry red wine
1 garlic clove, crushed
2 courgettes, sliced
1 yellow pepper, seeded and sliced
400g/14oz can chopped tomatoes
15ml/1 tbsp chopped fresh thyme
salt and black pepper
potato gratin, to serve

1 Preheat the oven to 180°C/350°F/ Gas 4. Lay the plaice skin-side down and, holding the tail end, push a sharp knife between the skin and flesh in a sawing movement. Hold the knife at a slight angle with the blade towards the skin.

3 Add the courgettes, yellow pepper, tomatoes and thyme and season to taste. Simmer for 3 minutes. Spoon the sauce into a large casserole.

4 Fold each fillet in half and put on top of the sauce. Cover and cook in the oven for 15–20 minutes, until the fish is opaque and flakes easily. Serve with a potato gratin.

2 Cut each onion into eight wedges. Put into a heavy-based saucepan with the stock. Cover and simmer for 5 minutes. Uncover and continue to cook, stirring occasionally, until the stock has reduced entirely. Add the wine and garlic clove to the pan and continue to cook until the onions are soft.

COOK'S TIP
Skinless white fish fillets such as plaice are low in fat and make an ideal tasty and nutritious basis for many low fat recipes such as this one.

NUTRITION NOTES	
Per portion:	
Energy	195Kcals/822kJ
Fat	3.8g
Saturated Fat	0.61g
Cholesterol	63mg
Fibre	2.2g

Monkfish and Mussel Skewers

Skinless white fish such as monkfish is a good source of protein whilst also being low in calories and fat. These attractive seafood kebabs, flavoured with a light marinade, are excellent grilled or barbecued and served with herby boiled rice and a mixed leaf salad.

INGREDIENTS

Serves 4

450g/1lb monkfish, skinned and boned
5ml/1 tsp olive oil
30ml/2 tbsp lemon juice
5ml/1 tsp paprika
1 garlic clove, crushed
4 turkey rashers
8 cooked mussels
8 raw prawns
15ml/1 tbsp chopped fresh dill
salt and black pepper
lemon wedges, to garnish
salad leaves and long grain and wild
  rice, to serve

1 Cut the monkfish into 2.5cm/1in cubes and place in a shallow glass dish. Mix together the oil, lemon juice, paprika and garlic clove and season.

2 Pour the marinade over the fish and toss to coat evenly. Cover and leave in a cool place for 30 minutes.

3 Cut the turkey rashers in half and wrap each strip around a mussel. Thread on to skewers, alternating with the fish cubes and raw prawns. Preheat the grill to high.

4 Grill the kebabs for 7–8 minutes, turning once and basting with the marinade. Sprinkle with chopped dill and salt. Garnish with lemon wedges and serve with salad and rice.

NUTRITION NOTES	
Per portion:	
Energy	145Kcals/604kJ
Fat	3.4g
Saturated Fat	0.81g
Cholesterol	84.7mg
Fibre	0.1g

BAKED COD WITH TOMATOES

For the very best flavour, use firm sun-ripened tomatoes for the sauce and make sure it is fairly thick before spooning it over the cod.

INGREDIENTS

Serves 4
10ml/2 tsp olive oil
1 onion, chopped
2 garlic cloves, finely chopped
450g/1lb tomatoes, peeled, seeded and chopped
5ml/1 tsp tomato purée
60ml/4 tbsp dry white wine
60ml/4 tbsp chopped flat leaf parsley
4 cod cutlets
30ml/2 tbsp dried breadcrumbs
salt and black pepper
new potatoes and green salad, to serve

NUTRITION NOTES

Per portion:
Energy	151Kcals/647kJ
Fat	1.5g
Saturated Fat	0.2g
Cholesterol	55.2mg
Fibre	2.42g

COOK'S TIP

For extra speed, use a 400g/14oz can of chopped tomatoes in place of the fresh tomatoes and 5–10ml/1–2 tsp ready-minced garlic in place of the garlic cloves.

1 Preheat the oven to 190°C/375°F/ Gas 5. Heat the oil in a pan and fry the onion for about 5 minutes. Add the garlic, tomatoes, tomato purée, wine and seasoning.

2 Bring the sauce just to the boil, then reduce the heat slightly and cook, uncovered, for 15–20 minutes until thick. Stir in the parsley.

3 Grease an ovenproof dish, put in the cod cutlets and spoon an equal quantity of the tomato sauce on to each. Sprinkle the dried breadcrumbs over the top.

4 Bake for 20–30 minutes, basting the fish occasionally with the sauce, until the fish is tender and cooked through, and the breadcrumbs are golden and crisp. Serve hot with new potatoes and a green salad.

PINEAPPLE CURRY WITH SEAFOOD

The delicate sweet and sour flavour of this curry comes from the pineapple, and although it seems an odd combination, it is delicious.

INGREDIENTS

Serves 4
600ml/1 pint/2½ cups coconut milk
30ml/2 tbsp red curry paste
30ml/2 tbsp fish sauce
15ml/1 tbsp sugar
225g/8oz king prawns, shelled and deveined
450g/1lb mussels, cleaned and beards removed
175g/6oz fresh pineapple, finely crushed or chopped
5 kaffir lime leaves, torn
2 red chillies, chopped, and coriander leaves, to garnish

1 In a large saucepan, bring half the coconut milk to the boil and heat, stirring, until it separates.

2 Add the red curry paste and cook until fragrant. Add the fish sauce and sugar and continue to cook for a few moments.

3 Stir in the rest of the coconut milk and bring back to the boil. Add the king prawns, mussels, pineapple and kaffir lime leaves.

4 Reheat until boiling and then simmer for 3–5 minutes, until the prawns are cooked and the mussels have opened. Remove any mussels that have not opened and discard. Serve garnished with chillies and coriander.

NUTRITION NOTES	
Per portion:	
Energy	187Kcals/793kJ
Fat	3.5g
Saturated Fat	0.53g
Cholesterol	175.5mg
Fibre	0.59g

CURRIED PRAWNS IN COCONUT MILK

A curry-like dish where the prawns are cooked in a spicy coconut-gravy with sweet and sour flavours from the tomatoes.

INGREDIENTS

Serves 4
600ml/1 pint/2½ cups coconut milk
30ml/2 tbsp Thai curry paste
15ml/1 tbsp fish sauce
2.5ml/½ tsp salt
5ml/1 tsp sugar
450g/1lb shelled king prawns, tails left intact and deveined
225g/8oz cherry tomatoes
1 chilli, seeded and chopped
juice of ½ lime, to serve
chilli and coriander, to garnish

1 Put half the coconut milk into a pan or wok and bring to the boil.

2 Add the curry paste to the coconut milk, stir until it disperses, then simmer for about 10 minutes.

3 Add the fish sauce, salt, sugar and remaining coconut milk. Simmer for another 5 minutes.

NUTRITION NOTES	
Per portion:	
Energy	184Kcals/778kJ
Fat	3.26g
Saturated Fat	0.58g
Cholesterol	315mg
Fibre	0.6g

4 Add the prawns, cherry tomatoes and chilli. Simmer gently for about 5 minutes until the prawns are pink and tender.

5 Serve sprinkled with lime juice and garnish with sliced chilli and chopped coriander leaves.

PRAWN NOODLE SALAD

A light, refreshing salad with all the tangy flavour of the sea. Instead of prawns, try squid, scallops, mussels or crab.

INGREDIENTS

Serves 4

115g/4oz cellophane noodles, soaked in
   hot water until soft
16 cooked prawns, peeled
1 small red pepper, seeded and cut into
   strips
1/2 cucumber, cut into strips
1 tomato, cut into strips
2 shallots, finely sliced
salt and black pepper
coriander leaves, to garnish

For the dressing

15ml/1 tbsp rice vinegar
30ml/2 tbsp fish sauce
30ml/2 tbsp fresh lime juice
pinch of salt
2.5ml/1/2 tsp grated fresh root ginger
1 lemon grass stalk, finely chopped
1 red chilli, seeded and finely sliced
30ml/2 tbsp roughly chopped mint
a few sprigs of tarragon, roughly chopped
15ml/1 tbsp snipped chives

1 Make the dressing by combining all the ingredients in a small bowl or jug; whisk well.

2 Drain the noodles, then plunge them in a saucepan of boiling water for 1 minute. Drain, rinse under cold running water and drain again well.

3 In a large bowl, combine the noodles with the prawns, red pepper, cucumber, tomato and shallots. Lightly season with salt and pepper, then toss with the dressing.

4 Spoon the noodles on to individual plates. Garnish with a few coriander leaves and serve at once.

NUTRITION NOTES

Per portion:

Energy	164.5Kcals/697kJ
Fat	2.9g
Saturated Fat	0.79g
Cholesterol	121mg
Fibre	1.86g

COOK'S TIP
Prawns are available ready-cooked and often shelled. To cook prawns, boil them for 5 minutes. Leave them to cool in the cooking liquid, then gently pull off the tail shell and twist off the head.

PASTA WITH TOMATO AND TUNA

INGREDIENTS

Serves 6

1 medium onion, finely chopped
1 celery stick, finely chopped
1 red pepper, seeded and diced
1 garlic clove, crushed
150ml/¼ pint/⅔ cup chicken stock
400g/14oz can chopped tomatoes
15ml/1 tbsp tomato purée
10ml/2 tsp caster sugar
15ml/1 tbsp chopped fresh basil
15ml/1 tbsp chopped fresh parsley
450g/1lb pasta shells
400g/14oz canned tuna in
   brine, drained
30ml/2 tbsp capers in vinegar, drained
salt and black pepper

1 Put the chopped onion, celery, red pepper and garlic into a pan. Add the stock, bring to the boil and cook for 5 minutes or until the stock has reduced almost completely.

2 Add the tomatoes, tomato purée, sugar and herbs. Season to taste and bring to the boil. Simmer for about 30 minutes until thick, stirring occasionally.

3 Meanwhile, cook the pasta in a large pan of boiling, salted water according to the packet instructions, until *al dente*. Drain thoroughly and transfer to a warm serving dish.

COOK'S TIP
If fresh herbs are not available, use a 400g/14oz can of chopped tomatoes with herbs and add 5–10ml/1–2 tsp mixed dried herbs, in place of the fresh herbs.

4 Flake the tuna fish into large chunks and add to the sauce with the capers. Heat gently for 1–2 minutes, pour over the pasta, toss gently and serve immediately.

NUTRITION NOTES

Per portion:

Energy	369Kcals/1549kJ
Fat	2.1g
Saturated Fat	0.4g
Cholesterol	34mg
Fibre	4g

VEGETABLES AND SALADS

Vegetables, as an accompaniment or as a main course, provide a tasty and nutritious choice at mealtimes. There are a huge array of fresh vegetables from around the world available all year so there's no excuse for not experimenting with new textures, colours and flavours. Choose from a wonderful selection of recipes, from delicious vegetarian main courses, such as Mixed Mushroom Ragoût, unusual side dishes like Courgette and Asparagus Parcels and Devilled Onions en Croûte, to light, flavourful salads, such as Marinated Cucumber Salad.

HERBY BAKED TOMATOES

INGREDIENTS

Serves 4–6

675g/1½ lb large red and yellow
   tomatoes
10ml/2 tsp red wine vinegar
2.5ml/½ tsp wholegrain mustard
1 garlic clove, crushed
10ml/2 tsp chopped fresh parsley
10ml/2 tsp snipped fresh chives
25g/1oz/½ cup fresh fine white
   breadcrumbs, for topping
salt and black pepper

NUTRITION NOTES

Per portion:

Energy	37Kcals/156kJ
Fat	0.49g
Saturated Fat	0.16g
Cholesterol	0
Fibre	1.36g

1 Preheat the oven to 200°C/400°F/
Gas 6. Thickly slice the tomatoes
and arrange half of them in a 900ml/
1½ pint/3¾ cup ovenproof dish.

COOK'S TIP
Use wholemeal breadcrumbs in
place of white, for added colour,
flavour and fibre. Use 5–10ml/
1–2 tsp mixed dried herbs, if fresh
herbs are not available.

2 Mix the vinegar, mustard, garlic
and seasoning together. Stir in
10ml/2 tsp cold water. Sprinkle the
tomatoes with half the parsley and
chives, then drizzle over half the
dressing.

3 Lay the remaining tomato slices on
top, overlapping them slightly.
Drizzle with the remaining dressing.

4 Sprinkle over the breadcrumbs.
Bake for 25 minutes or until the
topping is golden. Sprinkle with the
remaining parsley and chives. Serve
immediately, garnished with sprigs
of parsley.

POTATO GRATIN

The flavour of Parmesan is wonderfully strong, so a little goes a long way. Leave the cheese out altogether for an almost fat-free dish.

INGREDIENTS

Serves 4

1 garlic clove
5 large baking potatoes, peeled
45ml/3tbsp freshly grated Parmesan
  cheese
600ml/1 pint/2½ cups vegetable or
  chicken stock
pinch of grated nutmeg
salt and black pepper

1 Preheat the oven to 200°C/400°F/ Gas 6. Halve the garlic clove and rub over the base and sides of a large shallow gratin dish.

2 Slice the potatoes very thinly and arrange a third of them in the dish. Sprinkle with a little grated Parmesan cheese, and season with salt and pepper. Pour over some of the stock to prevent the potatoes from discolouring.

3 Continue layering the potatoes and cheese as before, then pour over the rest of the stock. Sprinkle with the grated nutmeg.

COOK'S TIP
For a potato and onion gratin, thinly slice one medium onion and layer with the potato.

4 Bake in the preheated oven for about 1¼–1½ hours or until the potatoes are tender and the tops well browned.

NUTRITION NOTES

Per portion:

Energy	190Kcals/802kJ
Fat	3.1g
Saturated Fat	1.60g
Cholesterol	7.5mg
Fibre	2.7g

DEVILLED ONIONS EN CROÛTE

Fill crisp bread cups with tender button onions tossed in a mustardy glaze. Try other low fat mixtures of vegetables, such as ratatouille, for a delicious change.

INGREDIENTS

Serves 4

12 thin slices of white or
*   wholemeal bread*
225g/8oz button onions or shallots
150ml/¼ pint/⅔ cup vegetable stock
15ml/1 tbsp dry white wine or
*   dry sherry*
2 turkey rashers, cut into thin strips
10ml/2 tsp Worcestershire sauce
5ml/1 tsp tomato purée
1.5ml/¼ tsp prepared English mustard
salt and black pepper
sprigs of flat leaf parsley, to garnish

1 Preheat the oven to 200°C/400°F/ Gas 6. Stamp out the bread into rounds with a 7.5cm/3in fluted biscuit cutter and use to line a 12–cup patty tin.

2 Cover each bread case with non-stick baking paper and fill with baking beans. Bake blind for 5 minutes. Remove the paper and beans and bake for a further 5 minutes, until lightly browned and crisp.

3 Meanwhile, put the button onions or shallots in a bowl and cover with boiling water. Leave for 3 minutes, then drain and rinse under cold water. Trim off their top and root ends and slip them out of their skins.

4 Simmer the onions and stock in a covered saucepan for 5 minutes. Uncover and cook, stirring occasionally until the stock has reduced entirely. Add all the remaining ingredients, except the flat leaf parsley, and cook for 2–3 minutes.

5 Fill the toast cups with the devilled onions. Serve hot, garnished with sprigs of flat leaf parsley.

NUTRITION NOTES	
Per portion:	
Energy	172Kcals/729kJ
Fat	1.5g
Saturated Fat	0.31g
Cholesterol	6.1mg
Fibre	1.7g

COURGETTE AND ASPARAGUS PARCELS

To appreciate the aroma, these paper parcels should be broken open at the table.

INGREDIENTS

Serves 4
2 medium courgettes
1 medium leek
225g/8oz young asparagus, trimmed
4 tarragon sprigs
4 whole garlic cloves, unpeeled
1 egg, beaten, to glaze
salt and black pepper

NUTRITION NOTES

Per portion:
Energy	52Kcals/215kJ
Fat	2.0g
Saturated Fat	0.43g
Cholesterol	48.1mg
Fibre	2.2g

1 Preheat the oven to 200°C/400°F/ Gas 6. Using a potato peeler, carefully slice the courgettes lengthways into thin strips.

2 Cut the leek into very fine julienne strips and cut the asparagus evenly into 5cm/2in lengths.

3 Cut out four sheets of greaseproof paper measuring 30 x 38cm/ 12 x 15in and fold in half. Draw a large curve to make a heart shape when unfolded. Cut along the inside of the line and open out.

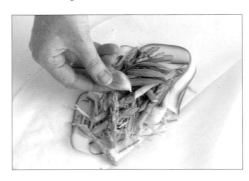

4 Divide the courgettes, asparagus and leek evenly between each paper heart, positioning the filling on one side of the fold line, and topping each with a sprig of tarragon and an unpeeled garlic clove. Season to taste.

5 Brush the edges lightly with the beaten egg and fold over.

6 Twist the edges together so that each parcel is completely sealed. Lay the parcels on a baking sheet and cook for 10 minutes. Serve immediately.

COOK'S TIP
Experiment with other vegetable combinations, if you like.

MIXED MUSHROOM RAGOÛT

These mushrooms are delicious served hot or cold and can be prepared up to two days in advance.

INGREDIENTS

Serves 4

1 small onion, finely chopped
1 garlic clove, crushed
5ml/1 tsp coriander seeds, crushed
30ml/2 tbsp red wine vinegar
15ml/1 tbsp soy sauce
15ml/1 tbsp dry sherry
10ml/2 tsp tomato purée
10ml/2 tsp soft light brown sugar
150ml/¼ pint/⅔ cup vegetable stock
115g/4oz baby button mushrooms
115g/4oz chestnut mushrooms,
    quartered
115g/4oz oyster mushrooms, sliced
salt and black pepper
coriander sprig, to garnish

NUTRITION NOTES

Per portion:
Energy	41Kcals/172kJ
Fat	0.7g
Saturated Fat	0.08g
Cholesterol	0
Fibre	1.0g

COOK'S TIP
There are many types of fresh mushrooms available and all are low in calories and fat. They add flavour and colour to many low fat dishes such as this tasty ragoût.

1 Put the first nine ingredients into a large saucepan. Bring to the boil and reduce the heat. Cover and simmer for 5 minutes.

2 Uncover the saucepan and simmer for 5 more minutes, or until the liquid has reduced by half.

3 Add the baby button and chestnut mushrooms and simmer for 3 minutes. Stir in the oyster mushrooms and cook for a further 2 minutes.

4 Remove the mushrooms from the pan with a slotted spoon and transfer them to a serving dish. Keep warm, if serving hot.

5 Boil the juices for about 5 minutes, or until reduced to about 75ml/ 5 tbsp. Season to taste.

6 Allow to cool for 2–3 minutes, then pour over the mushrooms. Serve hot or well chilled, garnished with a sprig of coriander.

Tofu and Green Bean Curry

This exotic curry is simple and quick to make. This recipe uses beans and mushrooms, but you can use almost any kind of vegetable such as aubergines, bamboo shoots or broccoli.

INGREDIENTS

Serves 4
350ml/12fl oz/1½ cups coconut milk
15ml/1 tbsp red curry paste
45ml/3 tbsp fish sauce
10ml/2 tsp sugar
225g/8oz button mushrooms
115g/4oz French beans, trimmed
175g/6oz bean curd, rinsed and cut
*   into 2cm/¾in cubes*
4 kaffir lime leaves, torn
2 red chillies, seeded and sliced
coriander leaves, to garnish

NUTRITION NOTES

Per portion:
Energy	100Kcals/420kJ
Fat	3.36g
Saturated Fat	0.48g
Cholesterol	0
Fibre	1.35g

1 Put about one third of the coconut milk in a wok or saucepan. Cook until it starts to separate and an oily sheen appears.

2 Add the red curry paste, fish sauce and sugar to the coconut milk. Mix together thoroughly.

3 Add the mushrooms. Stir and cook for 1 minute.

4 Stir in the rest of the coconut milk and bring back to the boil.

COOK'S TIP
Use 5–10ml/1–2 tsp hot chilli powder, if fresh red chillies aren't available. When preparing fresh chillies, wear rubber gloves and wash hands, work surfaces and utensils thoroughly afterwards. Chillies contain volatile oils which can irritate and burn sensitive areas, especially eyes.

5 Add the French beans and cubes of bean curd and simmer gently for another 4–5 minutes.

6 Stir in the kaffir lime leaves and chillies. Serve garnished with the coriander leaves.

CACHUMBAR

Cachumbar is a salad relish most commonly served with Indian curries. There are many versions; this one will leave your mouth feeling cool and fresh after a spicy meal.

INGREDIENTS

Serves 4

3 ripe tomatoes
2 chopped spring onions
1.5ml/¼ tsp caster sugar
salt
45ml/3 tbsp chopped fresh coriander

NUTRITION NOTES

Per portion:	
Energy	9.5Kcals/73.5kJ
Fat	0.23g
Saturated Fat	0.07g
Cholesterol	0
Fibre	0.87g

1 Remove the tough cores from the bottom of the tomatoes with a small sharp-pointed knife.

COOK'S TIP
Cachumbar also makes a fine accompaniment to fresh crab, lobster and shellfish.

2 Halve the tomatoes, remove the seeds and dice the flesh.

3 Combine the tomatoes with the spring onions, sugar, salt and chopped coriander. Serve at room temperature.

Marinated Cucumber Salad

Sprinkling cucumbers with salt draws out some of the water and makes them softer and sweeter.

Ingredients

Serves 6
2 medium cucumbers
15ml/1 tbsp salt
90g/3½oz/½ cup granulated sugar
175ml/6fl oz/¾ cup dry cider
15ml/1 tbsp cider vinegar
45ml/3 tbsp chopped fresh dill
pinch of pepper

Nutrition Notes

Per portion:
Energy	111Kcals/465kJ
Fat	0.1g
Saturated Fat	0.01g
Cholesterol	0
Fibre	0.62g

1 Slice the cucumbers thinly and place them in a colander, sprinkling salt between each layer. Put the colander over a bowl and leave to drain for 1 hour.

2 Thoroughly rinse the cucumber under cold running water to remove excess salt, then pat dry on absorbent kitchen paper.

Cook's Tip
As a shortcut, leave out the method for salting cucumber described in step 1.

3 Gently heat the sugar, cider and vinegar in a saucepan, until the sugar has dissolved. Remove from the heat and leave to cool. Put the cucumber slices in a bowl, pour over the cider mixture and leave to marinate for about 2 hours.

4 Drain the cucumber and sprinkle with the dill and pepper to taste. Mix well and transfer to a serving dish. Chill in the fridge until ready to serve.

CRACKED WHEAT AND MINT SALAD

INGREDIENTS

Serves 4

250g/9oz/1⅔ cups cracked wheat
4 tomatoes
4 small courgettes, thinly sliced
  lengthways
4 spring onions, sliced on the diagonal
8 ready-to-eat dried apricots, chopped
40g/1½oz/¼ cup raisins
juice of 1 lemon
30ml/2 tbsp tomato juice
45ml/3 tbsp chopped fresh mint
1 garlic clove, crushed
salt and black pepper
sprig of fresh mint, to garnish

1 Put the cracked wheat into a large bowl. Add enough boiling water to come 2.5cm/1in above the level of the wheat. Leave to soak for 30 minutes, then drain well and squeeze out any excess water in a clean dish towel.

2 Meanwhile, plunge the tomatoes into boiling water for 1 minute and then into cold water. Slip off the skins. Halve, remove the seeds and cores and coarsely chop the flesh.

3 Stir the chopped tomatoes, courgettes, spring onions, apricots and raisins into the cracked wheat.

4 Put the lemon and tomato juice, mint, garlic clove and seasoning into a small bowl and whisk together with a fork. Pour over the salad and mix well. Chill for at least 1 hour. Serve garnished with a sprig of mint.

NUTRITION NOTES

Per portion:

Energy	297Kcals/1245kJ
Fat	1.7g
Saturated Fat	0.27g
Cholesterol	0
Fibre	2.4g

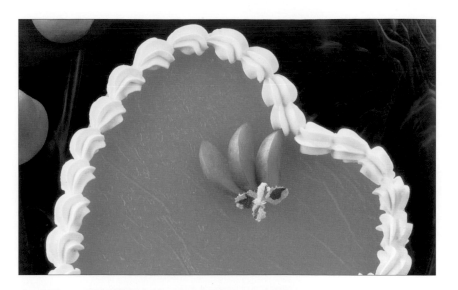

DESSERTS, CAKES AND BAKES

When we talk of desserts and cakes we tend to imagine deliciously rich, creamy, calorie-laden treats that are well out of reach for those who are following a low fat diet. However, with the right knowledge about low fat cooking methods it is very easy to create delicious, low fat desserts, cakes and bakes that are also full of flavour and appeal. Try desserts such as Banana, Maple and Lime Pancakes and Strawberry and Apple Crumble, refreshing Iced Oranges and delicious cakes and bakes, such as the classic Irish Whiskey Cake and Date and Apple Muffins.

STRAWBERRY AND APPLE CRUMBLE

A high-fibre, healthier version of the classic apple crumble. Raspberries can be used instead of strawberries, either fresh or frozen.

INGREDIENTS

Serves 4
450g/1lb cooking apples
150g/5oz/1¼ cups strawberries
30ml/2 tbsp granulated sugar
2.5ml/½ tsp ground cinnamon
30ml/2 tbsp orange juice
custard or yogurt, to serve

For the crumble
45ml/3 tbsp plain wholemeal flour
50g/2oz/⅔ cup porridge oats
25g/1oz/⅛ cup low fat spread

1 Preheat the oven to 180°C/350°F/ Gas 4. Peel, core and slice the apples. Halve the strawberries.

NUTRITION NOTES	
Per portion:	
Energy	182.3Kcals/785kJ
Fat	4g
Saturated Fat	0.73g
Cholesterol	0.5mg
Fibre	3.87g

2 Toss together the apples, strawberries, sugar, cinnamon and orange juice. Tip into a 1.2 litre/ 2 pint/5 cup ovenproof dish, or four individual dishes.

3 Combine the flour and oats in a bowl and mix in the low fat spread with a fork.

4 Sprinkle the crumble evenly over the fruit. Bake for 40–45 minutes (20–25 minutes for individual dishes), until golden brown and bubbling. Serve warm with custard or yogurt.

SULTANA AND COUSCOUS PUDDING

Most couscous on the market now is the pre-cooked variety, which needs only the minimum of cooking, but check the packet instructions first to make sure. Serve hot, with yogurt or skimmed-milk custard.

INGREDIENTS

Serves 4

50g/2oz/⅓ cup sultanas
475ml/16fl oz/2 cups apple juice
90g/3½oz/1 cup couscous
2.5ml/½ tsp mixed spice

1 Lightly grease four 250ml/8fl oz/ 1 cup pudding basins or one 1 litre/1¾ pint/4 cup pudding basin. Put the sultanas and apple juice in a pan.

2 Bring the apple juice to the boil, then cover the pan and leave to simmer gently for 2–3 minutes to plump up the fruit. Using a slotted spoon, lift out about half the fruit and put it in the bottom of the basin(s).

3 Add the couscous and mixed spice to the pan and bring back to the boil, stirring. Cover and leave over a low heat for 8–10 minutes, or until the liquid has been absorbed.

NUTRITION NOTES

Per portion:	
Energy	130.5Kcals/555kJ
Fat	0.40g
Saturated Fat	0
Cholesterol	0
Fibre	0.25g

4 Spoon the couscous into the basin(s), spread it level, then cover the basin(s) tightly with foil. Put the basin(s) in a steamer over boiling water, cover and steam for about 30 minutes. Run a knife around the edges, turn the puddings out carefully and serve.

COOK'S TIP

As an alternative, use chopped ready-to-eat dried apricots or pears, in place of the sultanas. Use unsweetened pineapple or orange juice in place of the apple juice.

BANANA, MAPLE AND LIME PANCAKES

Pancakes are a treat any day of the week, and they can be made in advance and stored in the freezer for convenience.

INGREDIENTS

Serves 4
115g/4oz/1 cup plain flour
1 egg white
250ml/8 fl oz/1 cup skimmed milk
50ml/2 fl oz/¼ cup cold water
sunflower oil, for frying

For the filling
4 bananas, sliced
45ml/3 tbsp maple syrup or golden syrup
30ml/2 tbsp lime juice
strips of lime rind, to decorate

1 Beat together the flour, egg white, milk and water until smooth and bubbly. Chill until needed.

2 Heat a small amount of oil in a non-stick frying pan and pour in enough batter just to coat the base. Swirl it around the pan to coat evenly.

3 Cook until golden, then toss or turn and cook the other side. Place on a plate, cover with foil and keep hot while making the remaining pancakes.

4 To make the filling, place the bananas, syrup and lime juice in a pan and simmer gently for 1 minute. Spoon into the pancakes and fold into quarters. Sprinkle with shreds of lime rind to decorate. Serve hot, with yogurt or low fat fromage frais.

COOK'S TIP
Pancakes freeze well. To store for later use, interleave them with non-stick baking paper, overwrap and freeze for up to 3 months.

NUTRITION NOTES

Per portion:

Energy	282Kcals/1185kJ
Fat	2.79g
Saturated fat	0.47g
Cholesterol	1.25mg
Fibre	2.12g

SPICED PEARS IN CIDER

Any variety of pear can be used for cooking, but it is best to choose firm pears for this recipe, or they will break up easily – Conference are a good choice.

Serves 4
4 medium firm pears
250ml/8 fl oz/1 cup dry cider
thinly pared strip of lemon rind
1 cinnamon stick
30ml/2 tbsp light muscovado sugar
5ml/1 tsp arrowroot
ground cinnamon, to sprinkle

1 Peel the pears thinly, leaving them whole with the stalks on. Place in a pan with the cider, lemon rind and cinnamon. Cover and simmer gently, turning the pears occasionally for 15–20 minutes, or until tender.

2 Lift out the pears. Boil the syrup, uncovered to reduce by about half. Remove the lemon rind and cinnamon stick, then stir in the sugar.

3 Mix the arrowroot with 15ml/1 tbsp cold water in a small bowl until smooth, then stir into the syrup. Bring to the boil and stir over the heat until thickened and clear.

4 Pour the sauce over the pears and sprinkle with ground cinnamon. Leave to cool slightly, then serve warm with low fat fromage frais.

COOK'S TIP
Whole pears look very impressive, but if you prefer, they can be halved and cored before cooking. This will shorten the cooking time slightly.

NUTRITION NOTES
Per portion:
Energy	102Kcals/428kJ
Fat	0.18g
Saturated fat	0.01g
Cholesterol	0
Fibre	1.65g

APRICOT DELICE

A fluffy mousse base with a layer of fruit jelly on top makes this dessert doubly delicious.

INGREDIENTS

Serves 8

2 x 400g/14oz cans apricots in natural juice
60ml/4 tbsp sugar
25ml/5 tbsp lemon juice
25ml/5 tsp powdered gelatine
425g/15oz low fat ready-to-serve custard
150ml/¼ pint/⅔ cup Greek-style yogurt
1 apricot, sliced, and fresh mint sprig, to decorate
whipped cream, to decorate (optional)

NUTRITION NOTES

Per portion:

Energy	130Kcals/547kJ
Fat	1.9g
Saturated Fat	1.11g
Cholesterol	3.7mg
Fibre	0.7g

COOK'S TIP

Use reduced fat Greek yogurt to cut calories and fat. Add the finely grated rind of 1 lemon to the mixture, for extra flavour. Peaches or pears are good alternatives to apricots.

1 Line the base of a 1.2 litre/2 pint/ 5 cup heart-shaped or round cake tin with non-stick baking paper.

2 Drain the apricots, reserving the juice. Put the apricots in a food processor or blender fitted with a metal blade, together with the sugar and 60ml/4 tbsp of the apricot juice. Blend to a smooth purée.

3 Measure 30ml/2 tbsp of the apricot juice into a small bowl. Add the lemon juice, then sprinkle over 10ml/ 2 tsp of the gelatine. Leave for about 5 minutes, until spongy.

4 Stir the gelatine into half of the purée and pour into the prepared tin. Chill in the fridge for 1½ hours, or until firm.

5 Sprinkle the remaining 15ml/3 tsp of gelatine over 60ml/4 tbsp of the apricot juice. Leave for about 5 minutes until spongy. Mix the remaining apricot purée with the custard, yogurt and gelatine. Pour on to the layer of set fruit purée and chill for 3 hours.

6 Dip the cake tin into hot water for a few seconds and unmould the delice on to a serving plate and peel off the lining paper. Decorate with the sliced apricot and mint sprig; for a special occasion, pipe whipped cream round the edge.

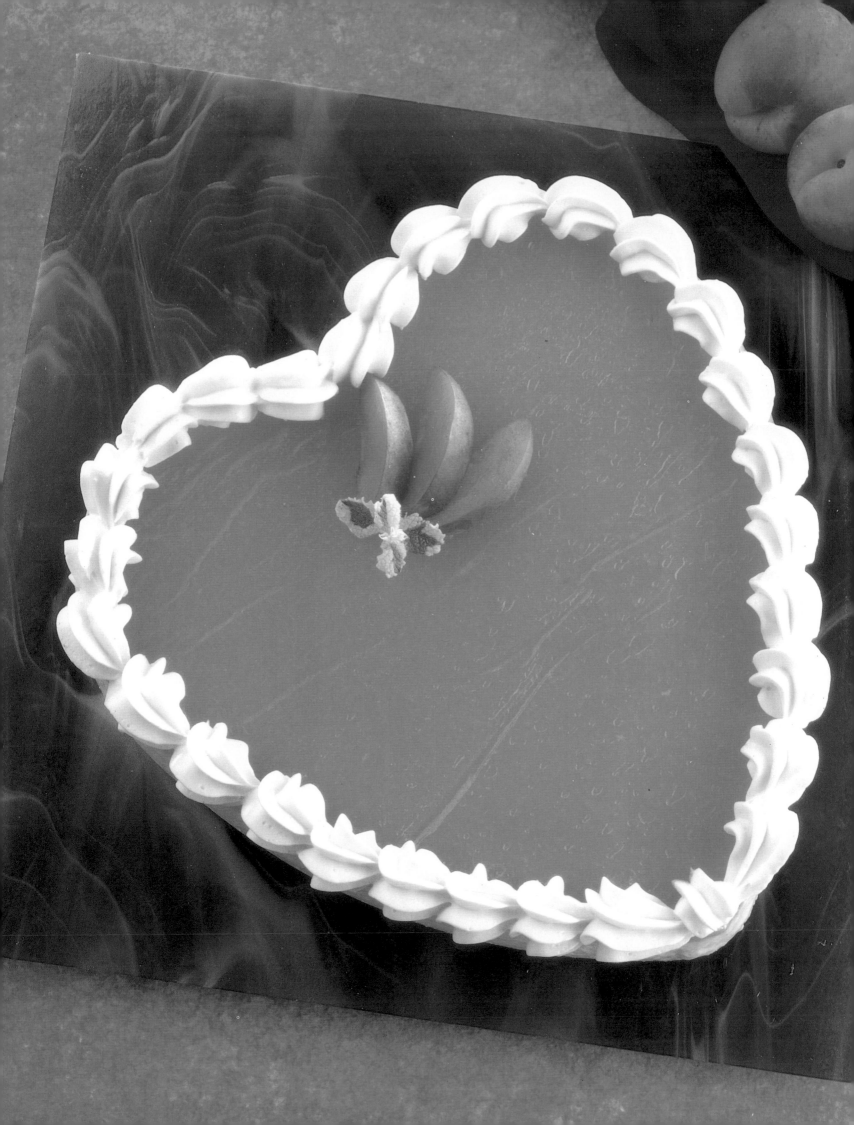

CRUNCHY FRUIT LAYER

INGREDIENTS

Serves 2

1 peach or nectarine
75g/3oz/1 cup crunchy toasted
  oat cereal
150ml/¼ pint/⅔ cup low fat
  natural yogurt
15ml/1 tbsp jam
15ml/1 tbsp fruit juice

NUTRITION NOTES

Per portion:

Energy	227Kcals/950kJ
Fat	2.7g
Saturated Fat	0.98g
Cholesterol	3.0mg
Fibre	3.6g

1 Remove the stone from the peach or nectarine and cut the fruit into bite-size pieces with a sharp knife.

2 Divide the chopped fruit between two tall glasses, reserving a few pieces for decoration.

3 Sprinkle the oat cereal over the fruit in an even layer, then top with the low fat yogurt.

4 Stir the jam and the fruit juice together in a jug, then drizzle the mixture over the yogurt. Decorate with the reserved peach or nectarine pieces and serve at once.

ICED ORANGES

The ultimate fat-free treat – these delectable orange sorbets served in fruit shells were originally sold in the beach cafés in the south of France.

INGREDIENTS

Serves 8
150g/5oz/⅔ cup granulated sugar
juice of 1 lemon
14 medium oranges
8 fresh bay leaves, to decorate

NUTRITION NOTES

Per portion:
Energy	139Kcals/593kJ
Fat	0.17g
Saturated Fat	0
Cholesterol	0
Fibre	3g

COOK'S TIP
Use crumpled kitchen paper to keep the shells upright.

1 Put the sugar in a heavy-based saucepan. Add half the lemon juice, then add 120ml/4fl oz/½ cup water. Cook over a low heat until the sugar has dissolved. Bring to the boil and boil for 2–3 minutes until the syrup is clear.

2 Slice the tops off eight of the oranges to make "hats". Scoop out the flesh of the oranges and reserve. Freeze the empty orange shells and "hats" until needed.

3 Grate the rind of the remaining oranges and add to the syrup. Squeeze the juice from the oranges, and from the reserved flesh. There should be 750ml/1¼ pints/3 cups. Squeeze another orange or add bought orange juice, if necessary.

4 Stir the orange juice and remaining lemon juice, with 90ml/6 tbsp water into the syrup. Taste, adding more lemon juice or sugar as desired. Pour the mixture into a shallow freezer container and freeze for 3 hours.

5 Turn the orange sorbet mixture into a bowl and whisk thoroughly to break up the ice crystals. Freeze for 4 hours more, until firm, but not solid.

6 Pack the mixture into the hollowed-out orange shells, mounding it up, and set the "hats" on top. Freeze the sorbet shells until ready to serve. Just before serving, push a skewer into the tops of the "hats" and push in a bay leaf, to decorate.

IRISH WHISKEY CAKE

This moist rich fruit cake is drizzled with whiskey as soon as it comes out of the oven.

INGREDIENTS

Serves 12

115g/4oz/²/₃ cup glacé cherries
175g/6oz/1 cup dark muscovado sugar
115g/4oz/²/₃ cup sultanas
115g/4oz/²/₃ cup raisins
115g/4oz/¹/₂ cup currants
300ml/¹/₂ pint/1¹/₄ cups cold tea
300g/10oz/2¹/₂ cups self-raising
   flour, sifted
1 egg
45ml/3 tbsp Irish whiskey

COOK'S TIP
If time is short, use hot tea and soak the fruit for just 2 hours.

1 Mix the cherries, sugar, dried fruit and tea in a large bowl. Leave to soak overnight until all the tea has been absorbed into the fruit.

NUTRITION NOTES

Per portion:	
Energy	265Kcals/1115kJ
Fat	0.88g
Saturated Fat	0.25g
Cholesterol	16mg
Fibre	1.48g

2 Preheat the oven to 180°C/350°F/ Gas 4. Grease and line a 1kg/2¹/₄lb loaf tin. Add the flour, then the egg to the fruit mixture and beat thoroughly until well mixed.

3 Pour the mixture into the prepared tin and bake for 1¹/₂ hours or until a skewer inserted into the centre of the cake comes out clean.

4 Prick the top of the cake with a skewer and drizzle over the whiskey while the cake is still hot. Allow to stand for about 5 minutes, then remove from the tin and cool on a wire rack.

ANGEL CAKE

A delicious light cake to serve as a dessert for a special occasion.

INGREDIENTS

Serves 10

40g/1½oz/⅓ cup cornflour
40g/1½oz/⅓ cup plain flour
8 egg whites
225g/8oz/1 cup caster sugar, plus extra
for sprinkling
5ml/1 tsp vanilla essence
90ml/6 tbsp orange-flavoured glacé
icing, 4–6 physalis and a little icing
sugar, to decorate

1 Preheat the oven to 180°C/350°F/ Gas 4. Sift both flours on to a sheet of greaseproof paper.

2 Whisk the egg whites in a large, clean, dry bowl until very stiff, then gradually add the sugar and vanilla essence, whisking until the mixture is thick and glossy.

3 Gently fold in the flour mixture with a large metal spoon. Spoon into an ungreased 25cm/10in angel cake tin, smooth the surface and bake for about 45–50 minutes, until the cake springs back when lightly pressed.

COOK'S TIP
If you prefer, omit the glacé icing and physalis and simply dust the cake with a little icing sugar – it is delicious to serve as a coffee-time treat, and also makes the perfect accompaniment to vanilla yogurt ice cream for a dessert.

4 Sprinkle a piece of greaseproof paper with caster sugar and set an egg cup in the centre. Invert the cake tin over the paper, balancing it carefully on the egg cup. When cold, the cake will drop out of the tin. Transfer it to a plate, spoon over the glacé icing, arrange the physalis on top and then dust with icing sugar and serve.

NUTRITION NOTES	
Per portion:	
Energy	139Kcals/582kJ
Fat	0.08g
Saturated Fat	0.01g
Cholesterol	0
Fibre	0.13g

COFFEE SPONGE DROPS

These are delicious on their own, but taste even better with a filling made by mixing low fat soft cheese with drained and chopped stem ginger.

INGREDIENTS

Makes 12
50g/2oz/½ cup plain flour
15ml/1 tbsp instant coffee powder
2 eggs
75g/3oz/6 tbsp caster sugar

For the filling
115g/4oz/½ cup low fat soft cheese
40g/1½oz/¼ cup chopped
 stem ginger

COOK'S TIP
As an alternative to stem ginger in the filling, try walnuts.

1 Preheat the oven to 190°C/375°F/ Gas 5. Line two baking sheets with non-stick baking paper. Make the filling by beating together the soft cheese and stem ginger. Chill until required. Sift the flour and instant coffee powder together.

NUTRITION NOTES

Per portion:
Energy	69Kcals/290kJ
Fat	1.36g
Saturated Fat	0.50g
Cholesterol	33.33mg
Fibre	0.29g

2 Combine the eggs and caster sugar in a bowl. Beat with a hand-held electric whisk until thick and mousse-like. (When the whisk is lifted, a trail should remain on the surface of the mixture for at least 15 seconds.)

3 Carefully add the sifted flour and coffee mixture and gently fold in with a metal spoon, being careful not to knock out any air.

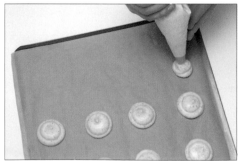

4 Spoon the mixture into a piping bag fitted with a 1cm/½in plain nozzle. Pipe 4cm/1½in rounds on the baking sheets. Bake for 12 minutes. Cool on a wire rack, then sandwich together with the filling.

DATE AND APPLE MUFFINS

You will only need one or two of these wholesome muffins per person, as they are very filling.

INGREDIENTS

Makes 12

150g/5oz/1¼ cups self-raising wholemeal flour
150g/5oz/1¼ cups self-raising white flour
5ml/1 tsp ground cinnamon
5ml/1 tsp baking powder
25g/1 oz/2 tbsp soft margarine
75g/3oz/½ cup light muscovado sugar
1 eating apple
250ml/8fl oz/1 cup apple juice
30ml/2 tbsp pear and apple spread
1 egg, lightly beaten
75g/3oz/½ cup chopped dates
15ml/1 tbsp chopped pecan nuts

1 Preheat the oven to 200°C/400°F/ Gas 6. Arrange 12 paper cake cases in a deep muffin tin. Put the wholemeal flour in a mixing bowl. Sift in the white flour with the cinnamon and baking powder. Rub in the margarine until the mixture resembles breadcrumbs, then stir in the muscovado sugar.

2 Quarter and core the apple, chop the flesh finely and set aside. Stir a little of the apple juice with the pear and apple spread until smooth. Mix in the remaining juice, then add to the rubbed-in mixture with the egg. Add the chopped apple to the bowl with the dates. Mix quickly until just combined.

3 Divide the mixture among the muffin cases.

4 Sprinkle with the chopped pecan nuts. Bake the muffins for 20–25 minutes until golden brown and firm in the middle. Remove to a wire rack and serve while still warm.

NUTRITION NOTES

Per muffin:

Energy	163Kcals/686kJ
Fat	2.98g
Saturated Fat	0.47g
Cholesterol	16.04mg
Fibre	1.97g

COOK'S TIP
Use a pear in place of the eating apple and chopped ready-to-eat dried apricots in place of the dates. Ground mixed spice is a good alternative to cinnamon.

PARMA HAM AND PARMESAN BREAD

This nourishing bread is almost a meal in itself.

INGREDIENTS

Serves 8

225g/8oz/2 cups self-raising wholemeal flour
225g/8oz/2 cups self-raising white flour
5ml/1 tsp baking powder
5ml/1 tsp salt
5ml/1 tsp black pepper
75g/3oz Parma ham
25g/1oz/2 tbsp freshly grated Parmesan cheese
30ml/2 tbsp chopped fresh parsley
45ml/3 tbsp Meaux mustard
350ml/12fl oz/1½ cups buttermilk
skimmed milk, to glaze

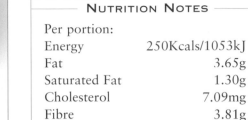

NUTRITION NOTES

Per portion:
Energy	250Kcals/1053kJ
Fat	3.65g
Saturated Fat	1.30g
Cholesterol	7.09mg
Fibre	3.81g

1 Preheat the oven to 200°C/400°F/ Gas 6. Flour a baking sheet. Place the wholemeal flour in a bowl and sift in the white flour, baking powder and salt. Add the pepper and the ham. Set aside about 15ml/1 tbsp of the grated Parmesan and stir the rest into the flour mixture with the parsley. Make a well in the centre.

2 Mix the mustard and buttermilk, pour into the flour and quickly mix to a soft dough.

3 Turn the dough on to a floured surface and knead briefly. Shape into an oval loaf, brush with milk and sprinkle with the Parmesan cheese. Put the loaf on the prepared baking sheet.

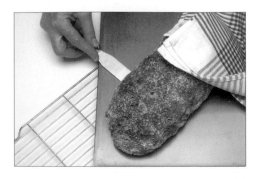

4 Bake the loaf for 25–30 minutes. Allow to cool before serving.

PEAR AND SULTANA TEABREAD

This is an ideal teabread to make when pears are plentiful – an excellent use for windfalls.

INGREDIENTS

Serves 6–8
25g/1oz/¼ cup rolled oats
50g/2oz/¼ cup light muscovado sugar
30ml/2 tbsp pear or apple juice
30ml/2 tbsp sunflower oil
1 large or 2 small pears
115g/4oz/1 cup self-raising flour
115g/4oz/¾ cup sultanas
2.5ml/½ tsp baking powder
10ml/2 tsp mixed spice
1 egg

1 Preheat the oven to 180°C/350°F/ Gas 4. Grease and line a 450g/1lb loaf tin with non-stick baking paper. Put the oats in a bowl with the sugar, pour over the pear or apple juice and oil, mix well and leave to stand for 15 minutes.

2 Quarter, core and coarsely grate the pear(s). Add to the oat mixture with the flour, sultanas, baking powder, mixed spice and egg, then mix together thoroughly.

3 Spoon the mixture into the prepared loaf tin and level the top. Bake for 50–60 minutes or until a skewer inserted into the centre comes out clean.

COOK'S TIP
Health food shops sell concentrated pear and apple juice, ready for diluting as required.

4 Transfer the teabread on to a wire rack and peel off the lining paper. Leave to cool completely.

NUTRITION NOTES

Per portion:
Energy	200Kcals/814kJ
Fat	4.61g
Saturated Fat	0.79g
Cholesterol	27.50mg
Fibre	1.39g

INDEX